World Geography

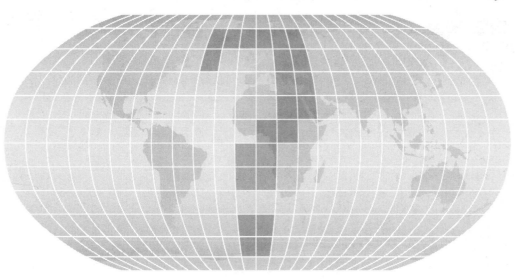

Where in the World Are You?

By
Leland Graham, Ph.D.
and Isabelle McCoy, M.Ed.

Carson-Dellosa Publishing Company, Inc.
Greensboro, North Carolina

Acknowledgements

The authors gratefully acknowledge the assistance and suggestions of the following persons:

Amy Alcorta, Valerie Crow, Chris McClellan, Sonny McCoy,
Johnny Ngyuen, Virginia Powell, John Spilane, and Connie York.

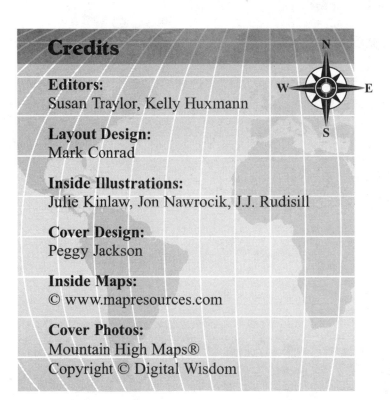

Credits

Editors:
Susan Traylor, Kelly Huxmann

Layout Design:
Mark Conrad

Inside Illustrations:
Julie Kinlaw, Jon Nawrocik, J.J. Rudisill

Cover Design:
Peggy Jackson

Inside Maps:
© www.mapresources.com

Cover Photos:
Mountain High Maps®
Copyright © Digital Wisdom

This book has been correlated to state, national, and Canadian provincial standards.
Visit *www.carsondellosa.com* to search for and view its correlations to your standards.

Table of Contents

Introduction

Due to phenomenal advances in communication and our world's interdependence, studying world geography is more important than ever. However, recent surveys have shown that people lack geographical knowledge about the earth on which they live. In fact, many people, including college students, have difficulty identifying countries on a world map or naming the oceans and continents. Can students identify the three largest countries in North America? Can they locate Egypt and Japan on a world map? Do they know the largest country in the world? In which country can they find people from the Ibo culture? Can they name the continents that border the Arctic Ocean? The answers to these and other questions can be found on your journey through *Where in the World Are You?* This book is designed to assist students in acquiring geographical knowledge about each continent and some of the countries located within that continent. The book is divided into seven informative profiles of the continents.

For each continent, the following is included:

- selected countries with basic information
- country's flag, government, land area, population, crops, mineral resources, landforms, and currency
- a political or physical map of each selected country
- activities, including various puzzles, charts and graphs, and recipes for foods native to that country or that are popular in that region
- a blackline flag is provided for coloring according to the description given on the country information page

The information and activities provided will stimulate students' interest in the world around them. The maps included on each country are large enough to be used by students for other class assignments. Students may locate and place additional cities, landmarks, and physical features on these maps. Indigenous spellings are used on some country maps. When a place is well known, it may be given in English so that it is meaningful to students. The annotated list of Web sites provides sources for additional research on particular countries and their customs, cultures, plant and animal life, historical information, and current environmental issues.

At the end of each continent section, there is an activity page concerning major landforms, environmental issues, an art activity, or a chart or graph comparing or contrasting selected countries within that particular continent. A ruler will be helpful for activities that require map scale and also for alignment when circling the words in the word searches. The culminating activity in this book has been designed for students to use their newly acquired knowledge to create a tour of the world as if they were travel agents.

The world geography skills test can be used as a pre-test and/or a post-test. The questions have been designed to sharpen or review a variety of geographic skills pertaining to the concepts in *Where in the World Are You?* The skills test will assess students' mastery of basic geography skills and help prepare them for success on standardized achievement tests.

The section at the end of this book includes a comprehensive glossary of key geographic terms and features. These words may be useful in reviewing and preparing for achievement tests. This vocabulary section can be used for reviewing geographical terms through the use of vocabulary and definition cards for use by individual students as well as in a class game format.

Physical Geography of North America

Location:

North America is located within the northern and western hemispheres. It is located north of South America, and is bordered to the north by the Arctic Ocean, to the east by the Atlantic Ocean, to the southeast by the Gulf of Mexico, and to the west by the Pacific Ocean. In addition to Canada, the United States, and Mexico, the North American continent includes the islands in the Caribbean, the countries in Central America, and the country Greenland.

Area:

North America is the third largest continent and has an area of 9,363,000 sq. mi. (24,249,000 sq km). The continent measures 4,000 miles (6,400 km) from east to west at its greatest distance. It measures 5,400 miles (8,900 km) from north to south at its greatest distance. Mount McKinley, with a height of 20,320 ft. (6,194 m), is North America's highest point. The lowest point is Death Valley, California and measures 282 ft. (86 m) below sea level.

Landforms:

Among the many landforms of North America are large lakes, plateaus, rivers, mountains, plains, basins, and islands. The Great Plains, a large, fairly dry area with fertile soil, stretches from Canada through west central United States. The eastern and southern coasts of the United States contain large coastal plains.

The islands of North America can be found mainly in the Caribbean and above the Arctic Circle. The Caribbean Islands are called the Greater Antilles and the Lesser Antilles. Greenland, Baffin, Ellesmere, and Victoria are four of the world's largest islands and are located above the Arctic Circle.

Numerous rivers flow across Canada and the United States. These rivers drain a huge area of North America. The Mississippi River, the largest river in the United States, provides shipping routes within the continent. In Canada, the Mackenzie River flows north 1,060 miles (1,600 km) into the Beaufort Sea. In Mexico, the Rio Grande forms part of the boundary between the United States and Mexico.

The Great Lakes are located along the border between the United States and Canada. One of these, Lake Superior, is the world's largest fresh water lake. In addition to providing important shipping routes, these lakes are valuable recreational resources.

From Alaska to Central America, high mountains run the length of North America. The Rocky Mountains stretch through Canada and the United States. The Appalachians, a chain of low mountains, are located on the eastern coast of the United States. The Sierra Madre Oriental is a range found in eastern Mexico.

In north central Mexico and the western part of the United States, there is a concentration of plateaus and basins. The Great Basin is located primarily in Nevada. The plateau areas of the North American continent are cut by canyons. The Grand Canyon in Arizona is just one example.

Climate:

North America is the only continent to have every kind of climate. The climate ranges from bitter cold temperatures in the Arctic to steamy heat in the tropics. Record temperatures have ranged from a high of 134° F (57° C) to a low of -87° F (-66° C).

Physical Map of North America

Directions: Match the following physical features of North America using the letters on the map below.

____ 1. Rocky Mountains   ____ 6. Great Plains   ____ 11. Lesser Antilles

____ 2. Gulf of Mexico   ____ 7. Mississippi River   ____ 12. Arctic Ocean

____ 3. Greater Antilles   ____ 8. Great Lakes   ____ 13. Caribbean Sea

____ 4. Rio Grande   ____ 9. Atlantic Ocean   ____ 14. Appalachian Mountains

____ 5. Pacific Ocean   ____ 10. Great Basin   ____ 15. Mount McKinley

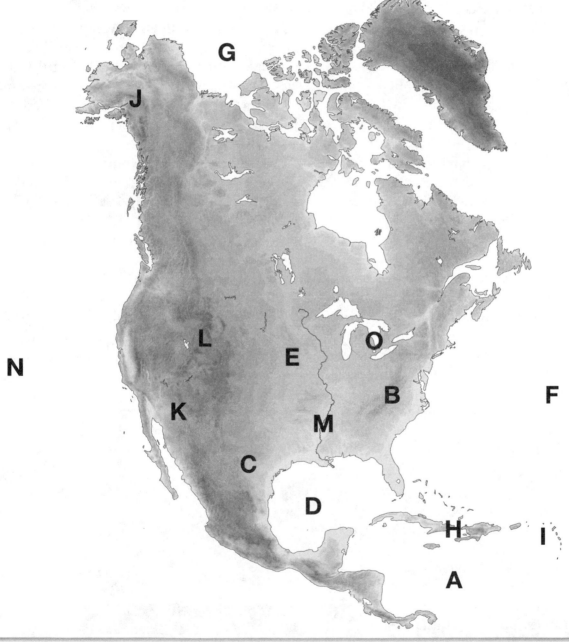

Where in the World Are You?

Capital: Ottawa

Largest Cities: Montreal, Toronto

Population: 32,207,113 (July 2003 estimate)

Land Area: 3,560,241 sq. mi. (9,220,970 sq km)

Highest Mountain: Mount Logan (19,551 ft./5,959 m)

Main Languages: English and French

Ethnic Groups: British, French, other European

Main Religions: Roman Catholic and Protestant

Government: Confederation with parliamentary democracy

Basic Currency: Dollar

This flag has three vertical stripes of red, white, and red with a red maple leaf in the center of the white strip.

You have arrived in the second largest country in the world in terms of area. Only Russia covers more land. This country extends across the continent of North America, from the province of Newfoundland on the Atlantic coast to the province of British Columbia on the Pacific coast. About 75% of the people live within 100 miles (150 kilometers) of the southern border. Much of the rest of the country is uninhabited or thinly populated because the country has rugged terrain and a severe climate.

The country is a federation (union) of 10 provinces and three territories. An independent and self-governing nation, this country still recognizes the British monarch, Queen Elizabeth II, as queen, symbolizing the country's historic ties to the United Kingdom.

A wide variety of geographic features—towering mountains, clear lakes, and lush forests—make this country a region of great natural beauty. Farther inland, fields of wheat and other grains cover vast prairies. These fertile farmlands contrast vividly with the Arctic lands to the north. Most of the nation's largest population centers and industrial areas are near the Great Lakes and the St. Lawrence River in the central part. In the east, fishing villages and sandy beaches dot the Atlantic coast.

Just like the landscape, the country's people are also varied. About one-third of the people have ancestors who came from England, Ireland, Scotland, or Wales. About one fourth have some French ancestry. The French, who live mostly in the province of Quebec, have kept the language and customs of their ancestors. Other large ethnic groups include Germans and Italians, and in the western part there are large numbers of Asians. Native peoples—American Indians and Inuit—make up a small percentage of the nation's population.

There is a wealth of natural resources in this country. In fact, European settlers first came to this country to fish in its coastal waters and to trap the fur-bearing animals in its forests. Later, the forests became sources of timber for shipbuilding and other construction. Today, pulpwood from these forests enables this country to lead the world in production of newsprint. Because of the fertile soil, this country ranks among the world's leading wheat producers. This country is also a leader in the generation of hydroelectric power because of numerous power plants on its rivers. Plentiful resources of petroleum, iron ore, and other minerals provide raw materials that help make this country a top manufacturing nation.

Where in the world are you?

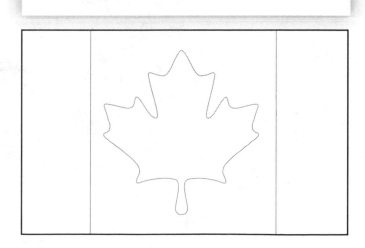

Political Map of Canada

Directions: First, correctly label the following provinces on the Canadian map. Then, using colored pencils or markers, lightly color each province and territory.

1. Yukon Territory
2. Newfoundland & Labrador
3. Ontario
4. Nunavut
5. Quebec

6. Nova Scotia
7. British Columbia
8. Prince Edward Island
9. Alberta
10. Saskatchewan

11. Manitoba
12. Northwest Territories
13. New Brunswick

Canadian Recipes

A variety of cultures can be found in the country of Canada. This contributes to various foods enjoyed by the Canadian people. Each region of Canada has its own specialties. In Quebec, the food is uniquely French-Canadian. Freshwater fish and moose meat are popular in the Northwest Territory. Seafood is the specialty in British Columbia and the Maritime Provinces, while beef is the main course in the Prairie Region.

Canadians consume more beef than any other meat. They also eat chicken, lamb, fish, and pork. Meals often include bread and potatoes. Besides potatoes, other favorites are beans, peas, carrots, and lettuce. Fruit pies, especially peach, blueberry, and apple, are among favorite desserts.

Salmon Cakes

Ingredients:

7 ¾ oz. (217 g) can salmon, drained and flaked
¼ cup (60 mL) fine, dry bread crumbs
2 eggs, slightly beaten
2 tablespoons (30 mL) lemon juice
¼ teaspoon (1 mL) pepper
vegetable cooking spray
½ cup (120 mL) finely chopped celery
¼ cup (60 mL) chopped green onions

Directions:

Combine salmon, bread crumbs, eggs, lemon juice, and pepper in a mixing bowl. Set aside. Spray non-stick skillet with cooking spray. Place over medium heat until hot. Add celery and onions; cook until tender. Add to salmon mixture. Mix well.

Coat skillet again with cooking spray. Place over medium-high heat until hot. For each salmon cake, scoop about ¼ cup mixture onto skillet. Shape into patty with a spatula. Cook about 3 minutes or until brown on each side. Serve immediately. Yield: 4 Cakes

Blueberry Muffins

Ingredients:

1 ¾ cups (420 mL) sifted all-purpose flour
¾ teaspoon (3 mL) salt
¼ cup (60 mL) sugar
2 teaspoons (10 mL) baking powder
2 eggs
2 (2-4) tablespoons (30-60 mL) melted butter
¾ cup (180 mL) milk
1 cup (240 mL) fresh blueberries

Directions:

Preheat oven to 400° F (200° C). Sift together flour, salt, sugar, and baking powder. Set aside. In a separate bowl, beat 2 eggs. Add melted butter and milk to the eggs. Combine the liquid and dry ingredients just until moist. Add blueberries to the batter. Fill well-greased muffin pans two-thirds full and bake 20 to 25 minutes. Yield: 2 dozen muffins

Capital: Mexico City
Largest Cities: Guadalajara, Monterrey
Population: 104,907,991 (July 2003 est.)
Land Area: 742,490 sq. mi. (1,923,040 sq km)
Highest Mountain: Volcan Pico de Orizaba (18,701 ft./5,700 m)
Main Languages: Spanish, Mayan, Nahuatl
Ethnic Groups: Mestizo (Amerindian-Spanish), Amerindian, White
Main Religion: Roman Catholic
Government: Federal Republic
Basic Currency: Peso

This flag has three vertical stripes of green, white, and red. In the center of the white stripe is the coat of arms.

Here you are in the third largest country in North America, and it is the largest Spanish-speaking country in the world. The Rio Grande River forms part of the border between this country and the United States. This country has 6,320 mi. (10,170 km) of coastline. The country's largest lake, Lake Chapala, is located close to the city of Guadalajara. The lake covers 417 sq. mi. (1,080 sq km).

There are a variety of landforms and climate regions found here. More than half of the land is covered with high mountains and plateaus. The Sierra Madre Occidental, a chain of mountains found in the west, has elevations exceeding 10,827 ft. (3,300 m). The Sierra Madre Oriental is located in the east, and rises to more than 13,120 ft. (4,000 m). Other landforms include plateaus, peninsulas, deserts, and rich farmland. The Chiapas Highlands have wide river valleys where many crops are grown, including coffee and fruits. Rain forests are located on the southern part of the Yucatan Peninsula. The climate in this country varies with the elevation of the land. Some mountain peaks are snow-covered year round. Other regions have long, hot summers and mild winters.

With abundant petroleum resources, this country is the fifth-leading exporter of oil in the world. This country leads the world as an exporter of silver. Gold, copper, lead, manganese, zinc, mercury, fluorite, and salt are also important products found here. The service industry, which includes tourism, banking, and advertising, is part of the fastest-growing section of the economy. About a fourth of the working population is employed in agriculture, forestry, or fishing. Maize (corn) is the leading crop. Most of the maize is used for making tortillas, which is an important food for most of the people in this country. This country is also a major producer of jojoba oil. The jojoba (pronounced hohoba) plant is found in the Sonoran Desert, which stretches from this country into southern Arizona.

Festivals or fiestas are still a popular way to celebrate holidays here. Often there are parades and dances included in these fiestas. There are several sports that are popular in this country, including baseball, jai alai, bullfights, and soccer, the most popular. Almost every large city has a bullring, including Mexico City, formerly known as Tenochtitlan, the ancient Aztec capital.

Where in the world are you?

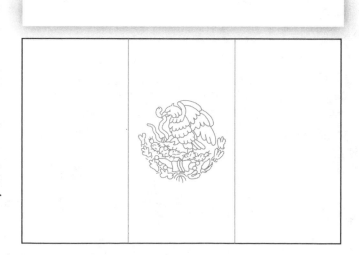

Political Map of Mexico

Directions: Use the map of Mexico to answer the questions. Circle the correct answers.

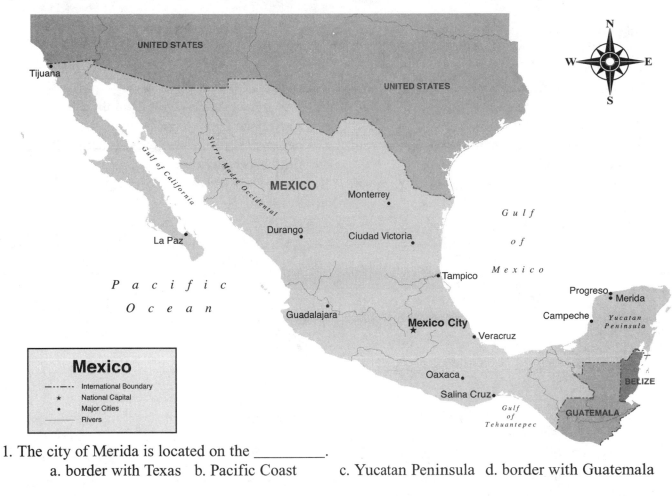

1. The city of Merida is located on the _____.
   a. border with Texas   b. Pacific Coast   c. Yucatan Peninsula   d. border with Guatemala

2. The Sierra Madre Occidental is located in the _____ part of Mexico.
   a. northwestern   b. northeastern   c. southwestern   d. southeastern

3. The Yucatan Peninsula is located _____ of Oaxaca.
   a. northeast   b. northwest   c. west   d. south

4. The city of _____ is not located along Mexico's Gulf Coast.
   a. Tampico   b. Veracruz   c. Progreso   d. Guadalajara

5. Durango is almost directly west of _____.
   a. Guadalajara   b. Ciudad Victoria   c. La Paz   d. Monterrey

6. The city of _____ is located on the Gulf of Tehuantepec.
   a. Progreso   b. Campeche   c. La Paz   d. Salina Cruz

Mexico Crossword Puzzle

Directions: Complete the puzzle using the clues below.

Across

3. peninsula off the southeast coast of Mexico
5. the most popular sport
6. desert in northwestern Mexico
8. the main religion of Mexico
11. river that forms part of the border between the United States and Mexico
12. highest point, Volcan Pico de _____

Down

1. Mexican city located just below California, USA
2. capital of Mexico
4. the ancient Aztec capital and the site of Mexico City
7. peninsula off the northwest coast of Mexico
9. the largest lake
10. festivals in Mexico

Where in the World Are You?

Capital: San José

Largest City: San José, Cartago

Population: 3,896,092 (July 2003 est.)

Land Area: 19,560 sq. mi. (50,660 sq km)

Highest Mountain: Cerro Chirripo (12,500 ft./3,810 m)

Main Language: Spanish, English

Ethnic Group: White (including Mestizo), Black, Amerindian, Chinese

Main Religion: Roman Catholic, Evangelical

Government: Democratic republic

Basic Currency: Colon

This flag has five horizontal bands of blue, white, red, white, and blue. To the left side of the wide red band is the coat of arms.

You have arrived in a small, mountainous country, situated between the countries of Nicaragua and Panama. The distance from north to south is 220 mi. (354 km), and it is 237 mi. (612 km) from east to west. Along the Caribbean Sea, it has 133 mi. (214 km) of coastline. Here, there are 380 mi. (612 km) of coastline along the Pacific Ocean. Through the center of the country is a chain of mountain ranges. These mountains divide the country into three main land regions, highlands, lowlands, and a coastal strip. The average annual rainfall ranges from 70 in. (180 cm) to 200 in. (510 cm) depending on location. The average temperature also varies according to the region, from 75° F (24° C) to 100° F (38° C).

The most valuable resource of this country is its rich volcanic soil. There have been over 200 volcanoes identified here and of those approximately 12 have been labeled as active. There are four volcanoes located near the capital city of San José. Two of those are active.

This country has traditionally had an agricultural-based economy; however, tourism and manufacturing are slowly overtaking agriculture to become the country's primary industries. The main crops are bananas, coffee, corn, and sugar cane. The people here are very hospitable, crime rates are low, and the scenery is spectacular. All of those factors have encouraged foreign tourists to visit this country in ever-increasing numbers. The country has become the world's fastest-growing destination for nature travel and adventure. Numerous cruise ships have made this country a regular port of call. Resorts are now emerging along both of the country's coastlines. A variety of activities are available for tourists. These activities include sports such as fishing, white-water rafting and diving, nature hikes, camping, bird watching, horseback riding, tennis, beach volleyball, and golf.

This country has the highest literacy rate (95%) of any country in Central America. The population is almost equally divided between rural and urban areas. Many people live in traditional adobe homes. Some wealthier people live in Spanish or ranch-style homes.

Where in the world are you?

Political Map of Costa Rica

Directions: Use the map of Costa Rica to answer the multiple choice questions. Circle the correct answer.

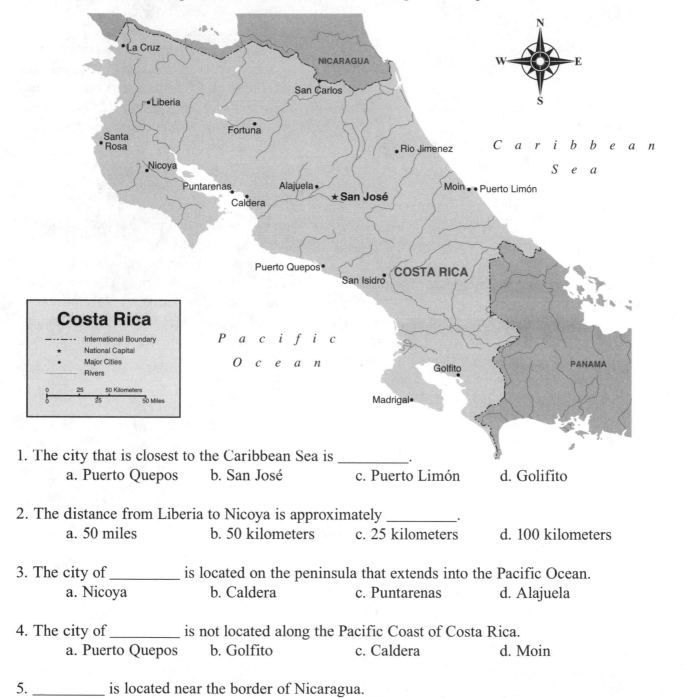

1. The city that is closest to the Caribbean Sea is _____.
   a. Puerto Quepos   b. San José   c. Puerto Limón   d. Golifito

2. The distance from Liberia to Nicoya is approximately _____.
   a. 50 miles   b. 50 kilometers   c. 25 kilometers   d. 100 kilometers

3. The city of _____ is located on the peninsula that extends into the Pacific Ocean.
   a. Nicoya   b. Caldera   c. Puntarenas   d. Alajuela

4. The city of _____ is not located along the Pacific Coast of Costa Rica.
   a. Puerto Quepos   b. Golfito   c. Caldera   d. Moin

5. _____ is located near the border of Nicaragua.
   a. San Isidro   b. Golfito   c. San José   d. San Carlos

6. The capital of Costa Rica is _____.
   a. Alajuela   b. San José   c. Caldera   d. San Isidro

Annual Production of Crops of Costa Rica

Directions: Use the chart to answer the questions. Circle the correct answers.

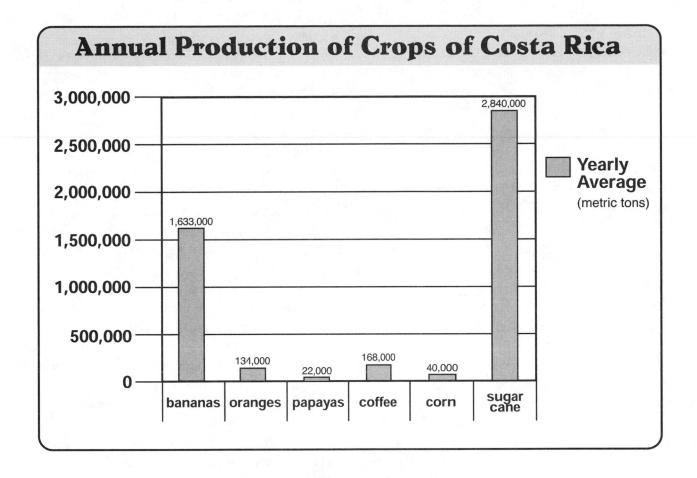

1. Costa Rica produces more _____ than bananas.
   a. oranges   b. coffee   c. sugar cane   d. corn

2. Costa Rica produces _____ more metric tons of coffee than oranges.
   a. 168,000   b. 34,000   c. 134,000   d. 22,000

3. The production of corn is _____ metric tons less than the production of oranges.
   a. 94,000   b. 134,000   c. 194,000   d. 40,000

4. Costa Rica produces less _____ than corn.
   a. sugar cane   b. oranges   c. papayas   d. coffee

5. The amount of sugar cane produced in Costa Rica is about _____ times the production of corn.
   a. 20   b. 7   c. 17   d. 71

Capital: Guatemala City
Largest Cities: Guatemala City, San Pedro
Population: 13,909,384 (July 2003 est.)
Land Area: 41,865 sq. mi. (108,430 sq km)
Highest Mountain: Volcan Tajumulco (13,816 ft./ 4,211 m)
Main Languages: Spanish, Amerindian
Ethnic Groups: Mestizo (mixed Amerindian-Spanish or Ladino), Amerindian (Mayan)
Main Religion: Roman Catholic, Protestant
Government: Constitutional democratic republic
Basic Currency: Quetzal

This flag has three vertical stripes of light blue, white, and light blue. The two blue stripes represent the Atlantic and Pacific Oceans. A coat of arms is centered on the white stripe.

This country has more people than any other Central American country. Most of the people live in the rugged mountains in the central part of the country. On a high plateau lies Guatemala City, the capital and industrial center of the country. Almost half of the people are Indians, whose way of life differs greatly from that of other inhabitants of the country. Today, the Indians live in peasant or farm communities apart from the main life of the country. Most speak Indian languages and wear traditional Indian clothing. Most of the other residents—called Ladinos—are of mixed Indian and Spanish ancestry. They speak Spanish and follow a form of Spanish-American customs. The Ladinos include peasants and laborers as well as people in cities and towns who control the government.

With a tropical climate, the temperatures vary according to altitude. The plains and lowlands have an average yearly temperature of 80° F (27° C). Mountain valleys 4,000 to 6,000 ft. (1,200 to 1,800 m) above sea level average 60° to 70° F (16° to 21° C). The higher valleys sometimes have frost, and average 40° F (4° C). The rainy season lasts from May to November. Rainfall amounts range from 20 to 30 in. (51 to 76 cm) annually in the eastern highlands to 80 to 150 in. (200 to 381 cm) annually in the northern plain.

Being a developing country, its major natural resource is fertile soil. Thick forests cover almost half the land. The country's main sources of income are exported farm products, particularly coffee, sugar, bananas, and a spice called cardamom. Coffee represents 30% of these exports. Corn is the basic food of most inhabitants and the chief crop grown for use within the country. Other important food crops include beans, rice, and wheat.

Children between the ages of seven and thirteen are required to attend school, with about 55% actually attending primary school. Only about 15% attend high school. School attendance is much higher among Ladinos in the city than it is among Indians in the rural areas.

Soccer, basketball, and volleyball are the most popular sports. For Ladino and Indian peasants, religious festival days provide the main sources of recreation. These holidays include religious processions, fireworks, and the country's famous marimba music. In the Indian communities, the people also perform dances that represent events from history or legends.

Where in the world are you?

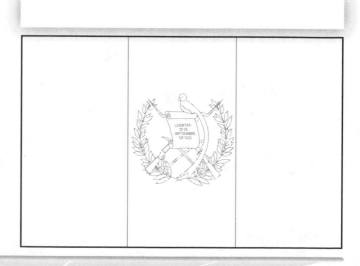

Guatemala Political Map

Directions: Use the map of Guatemala to answer the questions. Circle the correct answers.

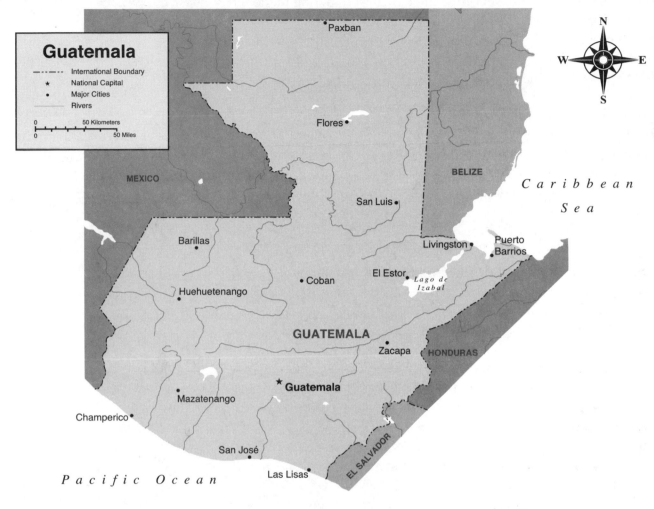

1. The distance from Guatemala City to Barillas is approximately _____ miles.
   a. 50   b. 100   c. 75   d. 150

2. Lago de Izabal is closer to _____ than to Coban.
   a. Flores   b. Champerico   c. Mazatenango   d. Puerto Barrios

3. All of the following are on Guatemala's Pacific Coast except _____.
   a. Las Lisas   b. San José   c. Champerico   d. Zacapa

4. Flores is _____ of Zacapa.
   a. north   b. south   c. east   d. west

5. The bordering country closest to the city of Zapaca is _____.
   a. Mexico   b. El Salvador   c. Honduras   d. Belize

Decoding Guatemala

Directions: Can you guess this Spanish greeting? Answer the questions using the key below and then fill in the blanks at the bottom of the page by unscrambling the letters.

1. Highest mountain __ O __ O __ __ __ __ __

2. The country's currency __ __ O __ __ __ __

3. Capital city of Guatemala O __ __ __ __ __ __ __ __ __ __ __ __

4. People of mixed Spanish and Indian ancestry __ __ O __ __ __ __

5. A spice grown in Guatemala __ __ __ __ O __ O

6. One of the most popular sports O __ __ __ __ __

7. The type of climate found in Guatemala __ __ __ __ O __ __ __

8. This lasts from May to November __ __ __ O __ __ __ __ O __ __

9. Thirty percent of the total exports come from this product. __ O __ __ __ __

10. The basic food of the Guatemalan people __ O __ __

11. Famous music played during holidays __ __ __ O __ O __

12. From the ages of 7 to 13, children must attend O __ __ __ __ __

“ __ __ __ __ __ __ __ __ __ __ __ __ __ __ __ __ __ __ !”

Where in the World Are You?

Capital: Kingston
Largest Cities: Kingston, Montego Bay
Population: 2,695,867 (July 2003 est.)
Land Area: 4,182 sq. mi. (10,831 sq km)
Highest Mountain: Blue Mountain (7,402 ft./2,256 m)
Main Languages: English, Creole
Ethnic Groups: Black, East Indian
Main Religions: Protestant, Roman Catholic
Government: Constitutional parliamentary democracy
Basic Currency: Dollar

The flag has a gold diagonal cross with black triangles on the hoist and fly sides and green triangles at the top and bottom. Gold, black, and green represent sunlight, hardships, hope, and agricultural wealth.

The third largest island in the Caribbean Sea, this island is located in the West Indies. Only Cuba and Hispaniola are larger. At its greatest distances, the island measures only 51 mi. (82 km) from north to south and 146 mi. (235 km) from east to west. This island has three land regions: coastal plains, central hills and plateau, and eastern mountains—the Blue Mountains. In the northwestern region, there are many limestone formations, including many deep depressions, called cockpits. This is the reason that the area is sometimes called "Cockpit Country."

When Christopher Columbus arrived on this island in 1494, he met the Arawak Indians. The Spanish enslaved the Arawak people and later brought Africans to the island as slaves. Disease and overwork killed most of the Arawak people. In the 1670's, the island was used as a base by British pirates in order to attack Spanish ships and ports.

The tropical climate of this country is cooled by the winds blowing in from the Caribbean Sea.

Temperatures range from about 75° F (24° C) in the winter to about 80° F (27° C) in the summer; however, temperatures in the mountains may drop to 40° F (4° C). The rainy seasons extend from May through June and then from September through November. Rainfall varies from 30 in. (76 cm) near the coast to about 200 in. (510 cm) in the mountains. Because of the pleasant climate, beautiful beaches, and splendid mountains, this island attracts over 850,000 tourists each year.

The food consumed in this country is usually very spicy. These foods include fish, rice with beans, and stews. A very popular food is jerk, which consists of roasted, spicy pieces of barbecued chicken or pork. Beverages consumed with meals include coffee, fruit juices, herbal teas, and drinks made from boiled roots.

Cricket, field hockey, soccer, tennis, and track and field are popular sports. Reggae and calypso are the most popular forms of music and dance. A grand festival celebrated in the spring is Carnival, which includes parades, costumes, and parties. This celebration is similar to Mardi Gras festival of New Orleans, Louisiana in the United States.

Where in the world are you?

Jamaican Political Map

Directions: Use the map of Jamaica to answer the questions. Circle the correct answers.

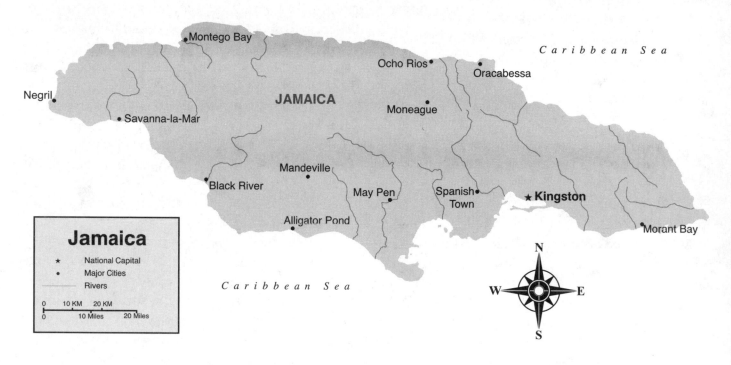

1. The distance from Ocho Rios to Oracabessa is approximately _____.
   a. 10 kilometers   b. 10 miles   c. 20 miles   d. 30 kilometers

2. The capital of Jamaica is _____.
   a. Mandeville   b. Negril   c. Kingston   d. Spanish Town

3. All of the following cities are located along the coast except _____.
   a. Black River   b. Savanna-la-Mar   c. Mandeville   d. Negril

4. Montego Bay is almost directly north of _____.
   a. Alligator Pond   b. Black River   c. Spanish Town   d. Kingston

5. May Pen is closer to _____ than to Ocho Rios.
   a. Negril   b. Spanish Town   c. Montego Bay   d. Morant Bay

Jamaica Word Search

Directions: Find and circle the hidden words in the puzzle below.

```
A V H C B T O G Y P A N B C Z V R B M R
C J L R S O Y I R V K L A E I H R C O A
Y O A X Y A W L D Z U L A U V N A W N I
S I A W U D X V F E Y G Y Y S G I D T N
T U L S A D Y J M P G S S K X Z S A E Y
E U Y F T K F O S E A U T Y R U P N G S
M Y C P O A U O R P U V C I P T X X O E
T C C U F N L P P Q A R V Y N M D S B A
J T F R T G L P Y P E M M K S N N R A S
D N M A R A L K L X T U L E P U O L Y O
R T I Z T N J W H A J E U I I N T A G N
S N Z E H N E T N B I O B Z E Q S V B C
S P A V V N E S L S E N C W E S G I T C
D U Q F M R P U A Y P E S T P X N N V X
K S I M F V W F B II D R X J E K I R A X
G E X Z Z Q F H O G V C R K B K K A S N
V U Y H J V M U S T I P K C O C C C P K
S P I C Y F O O D R V Q F G G W Z I D V
I O D R X J A S K A W A R A K R E J R U
C A R I B B E A N S E A H U G O O T S C
```

ARAWAK	BLUE MOUNTAINS	COCKPITS
CRICKET	COASTAL PLAINS	CARIBBEAN SEA
CALYPSO	RAINY SEASON	MONTEGO BAY
KINGSTON	SPICY FOOD	REGGAE
PLATEAU	CARNIVAL	JERK

North America Crossword

Directions: Use pages 5-20 and other available resources to complete the crossword puzzle.

Across

1. Capital of Mexico
5. Largest mountain system in North America
7. Chain of Caribbean Islands which includes Jamaica, Cuba, Hispaniola, and Puerto Rico
9. Tallest mountain in North America
12. Lowest elevation in North America

Down

2. River that begins in the Canadian Mountains and crosses Alaska before emptying into the Bering Sea
3. Colorful desert land in Arizona
4. Largest river in the United States
6. Longest river in Canada
8. Largest fresh water lake in the world
10. River that begins in the Rocky Mountains and flows to the Gulf of Mexico
11. Capital city of Canada

Physical Geography of South America

Location:

South America is located south of North America and to the north of Antarctica. It is bordered by the Atlantic Ocean on the east, by the Pacific Ocean on the west, and by the Caribbean Sea to the north. The entire continent is located in the western hemisphere. Most of it is located south of the equator. The Isthmus of Panama connects South America to Central and North America.

Area:

South America, with an area of approximately 6,900,000 sq. mi. (17,800,000 sq km), is the fourth largest continent. The continent measures 4,750 miles (7,645 km) from north to south, and it measures 3,200 mi. (5,150 km) from east to west. Valdes Peninsula is the lowest point on the continent and has an elevation of 131 ft. (40 m) below sea level. The highest point is Mount Aconcagua with an elevation of 22,831 ft. (6,959 m).

Landforms:

Among the many dramatic features of South America are mountains, rivers, rain forests, deserts, waterfalls, and plains. The Andes Mountains extend for approximately 4,500 mi. (7,200 km) from Venezuela in the north to Tierra del Fuego in the south. They are the world's longest mountain range above sea level.

There are five large river systems in South America. The longest of these, the Amazon, is the world's second longest river. The Amazon carries one-fifth of the world's fresh river water. More than one-third of South America is covered by rain forests. Most of the Amazon River Basin is occupied with dense rain forests, which provide many valuable forest products. The continent's largest lake, Lake Maracaibo, covers 5,217 sq. mi. (13,512 sq km). The highest navigable lake in the world, Lake Titicaca, is located in the Andes on the border between Bolivia and Peru.

Many spectacular waterfalls can be found in South America. The highest waterfall, Angel Falls, is located in Venezuela. It plunges 3,212 ft. (979 m) over a cliff, creating a heavy mist and draining into the Churun River. On the border between Argentina and Brazil, the Iguaçu Falls is considered by many to be the most wonderful natural sight in South America.

The Central Plains cover about three-fifths of South America. They are composed of the Llanos, the Selva, the Gran Chaco, and the Pampa. All of them are drained by huge river systems that empty into the Atlantic Ocean.

Climate:

The continent of South America has a wide variety of climates. They vary from heavy rainfall along the southwest coast to dry regions in the Atacama Desert in Chile. Two of the driest regions on the continent are the Atacama Desert and Patagonia. Arica, a northern port city in Chile, receives an average of only 3/100 inch (0.76 mm) of rain a year. The plateaus of Patagonia receive only about 10 inches (25 cm) a year.

The tropical rain forest in the Amazon River Basin is steamy while the snow-capped Andes Mountains are icy cold. Although the Andes are always cold, most of the continent has warm weather year-round.

Political Map of South America

Directions: Match the letters on the map of South America with the countries listed below.

_____ 1. Venezuela

_____ 2. French Guiana

_____ 3. Colombia

_____ 4. Ecuador

_____ 5. Guyana

_____ 6. Suriname

_____ 7. Peru

_____ 8. Brazil

_____ 9. Bolivia

_____ 10. Paraguay

_____ 11. Argentina

_____ 12. Uruguay

_____ 13. Chile

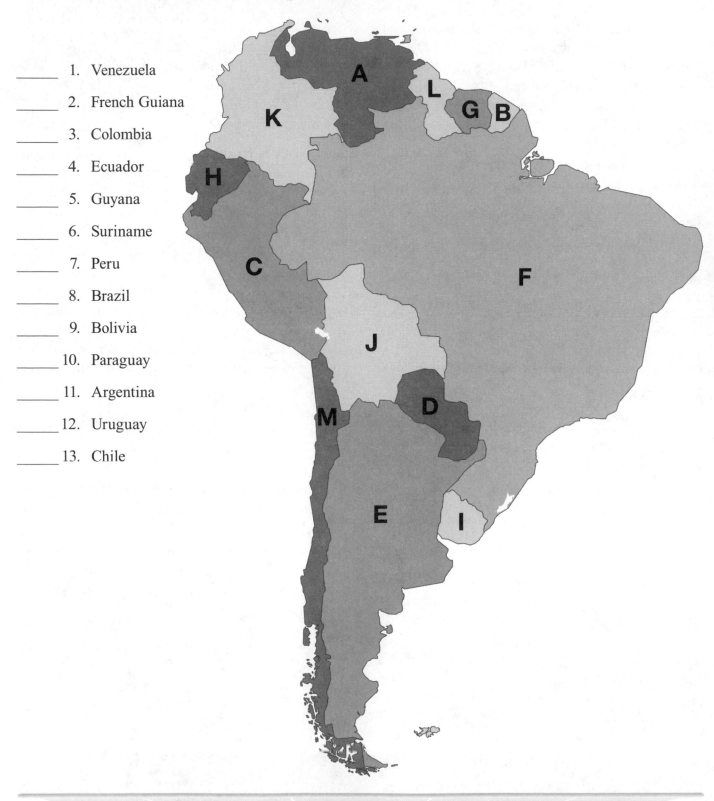

Where in the World Are You?

Capital: Caracas

Largest Cities: Caracas, Maracaibo, Valencia

Population: 24,654,694 (Est. 2003)

Land Area: 340,561 sq. mi. (882,050 sq km)

Highest Mountain: Pico Bolivar (16,430 ft./5,007 m)

Main Languages: Spanish

Ethnic Groups: Spanish, Italian, Portuguese, Arab, German, African

Main Religions: Roman Catholic

Government: Federal republic

Basic Currency: Bolivar

The flag has three horizontal stripes of yellow, blue, and red. The arc of seven white stars is centered on the blue stripe. Although some representations of the Venezuelan flag consist of the three stripes and seven stars, most contain a representation of the country's coat of arms in the upper hoist-side corner.

This country, which lies on the north coast of South America, measures 790 mi. (1,271 km) from north to south and 925 mi. (1,489 km) from east to west at its greatest distance. Along the Caribbean Sea and the North Atlantic Ocean, it has 1,750 mi. (2,816 km) of coastline. Mountain ranges extend across much of the northern part of this country, which is the country's most densely populated region. Caracas, the capital and largest city, lies in this region.

The country has four major land regions: 1) The Maracaibo Basin lies in the northwestern section and consists of Lake Maracaibo, the largest lake in South America, and the lowlands around it. The continent's largest known petroleum deposits lie in the Maracaibo Basin. 2) The Andean Highlands begin southwest of the Maracaibo Basin and extend across the northern part of the country. Most of the country's people live in this region. 3) The vast grassy plains region, the Llanos, lies between the Andean Highlands and the Guiana Highlands.

The Orinoco River, the longest river in the country, flows from west to east along the southern border of the Llanos. 4) The Guiana Highlands rise south of the Llanos and cover nearly half of the country. Angel Falls, the world's highest waterfall, plunges 3,212 ft. (979 m) in the Guiana Highlands.

Traditional foods include black beans, a type of banana called plantains, and rice, which are usually eaten with beef, pork, poultry, or fish. The traditional bread is round corn-meal cake called arepa. The national dish of this country is hallaca, which is served mainly at Christmas. Hallacas consist of corn-meal dough filled with a variety of foods and cooked in wrappers.

Baseball and soccer are the most popular spectator sports. Professional teams play before large crowds in city stadiums. Several cities have bullfights, but they do not attract as many people as competitive sports. The people of this country also enjoy music and dancing. Popular dances include the exciting and lively Caribbean dances such as the merengue and guaracha. The national folk dance of the country is joropo, a stamping dance performed to music of cautros (four-stringed guitars), the harp, and maracas. Rock music is also very popular among the young citizens of this country.

Where in the world are you?

Political/Physical Map of Venezuela

Directions: Use the map of Venezuela to answer the questions. Circle the correct answers.

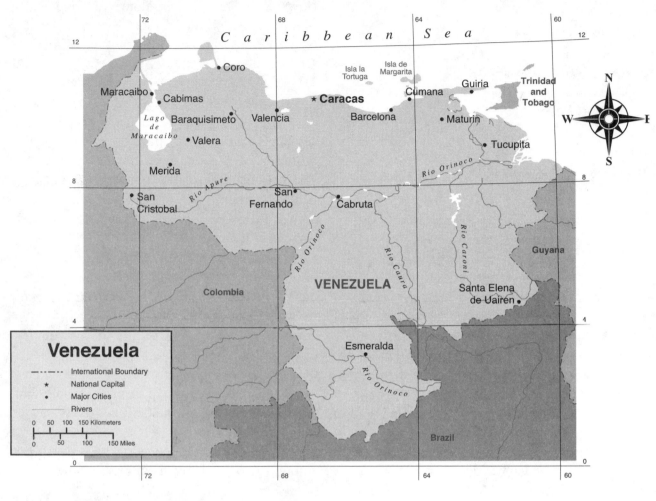

1. On what river is the city of San Cristobal located?
   a. Rio Caura   b. Rio Orinoco   c. Rio Apure   d. Rio Caroni

2. The city of _____ is located near Lago de Maracaibo (Lake Maracaibo).
   a. Barcelona   b. Cabimas   c. Caracas   d. Maturin

3. The distance from Merida to San Cristobal is approximately _____.
   a. 150 kilometers   b. 375 kilometers   c. 375 miles   d. 150 miles

4. San Fernando is located at approximately _____ degrees north latitude.
   a. 4   b. 8   c. 60   d. 64

5. Valencia is almost directly west of _____.
   a. San Fernando   b. Valera   c. Coro   d. Barcelona

Venezuelan Fun Facts

Directions: Match the following "fun facts" with their descriptions.

_____ 1. Caracas

_____ 2. Llanos

_____ 3. baseball

_____ 4. Cautro

_____ 5. plantains

_____ 6. Arepa

_____ 7. Maracaibo

_____ 8. merengue

_____ 9. Hallaca

_____ 10. Orinoco River

_____ 11. Angel Falls

_____ 12. Joropo

_____ 13. Venezuelan flag

_____ 14. Roman Catholic

_____ 15. Pico Bolivar

A. a type of banana that is a traditional food

B. the world's highest waterfall

C. one of the most popular spectator sports

D. the longest river in Venezuela

E. It has three horizontal stripes of yellow, blue and red.

F. the highest mountain in Venezuela

G. the capital and largest city

H. four-stringed guitar

I. vast plains that spread across central Venezuela

J. largest lake in South America

K. the main religion of Venezuela

L. the national folk dance of the country

M. national dish of Venezuela

N. the traditional bread

O. Two lively and exciting Caribbean dances are the guaracha and the _____.

Where in the World Are You?

Capital: Buenos Aires
Largest Cities: Buenos Aires, Córdoba, Rosario
Population: 38,740,807 (July 2003 est.)
Land Area: 1,056,641 sq. mi. (2,736,690 sq km)
Highest Mountain: Cerro Aconcagua (22,835 ft./ 6,960 m)
Main Languages: Spanish, English, Italian, German, French
Ethnic Groups: White (Spanish and Italian), Mestizo, Amerindian
Main Religion: Roman Catholic
Government: Republic
Basic Currency: Peso

The flag has three equal horizontal stripes of light blue on the top and bottom with white in the middle. In the center of the white stripe is a yellow sun with a human face.

You have arrived in South America's second largest country in both area and population and the eighth largest country in the world in size. From north to south, the country measures 2,300 mi. (3,700 km), and it measures 980 mi. (1,577 km) from east to west. Along the Atlantic Ocean, this country has 2,940 mi. (4,731 km) of coastline. At the southern tip, the country is only about 600 mi. (970 km) from the continent of Antarctica.

There are four main land regions including Patagonia, the Andine, the Pampa, and Northern. Patagonia, the southern region, contains dry, windy plateaus. It takes up about a fourth of the land but less than 3% of the people live there. This land is not arable due to the poor soil quality and lack of adequate rainfall. The Andine is the mountainous area in the western region where the Piedmont area and the Andes Mountains are located. The northern region contains two parts, Gran Chaco and Mesopotamia. The Gran Chaco contains forested plains. During the summer, heavy rains cause flooding; however, during the rest of the year the region is stricken with drought. Mesopotamia is a fertile region located between two rivers, the Paraná and the Uruguay.

Manufacturing is the main component of the economy. About one-fourth of the labor force is employed in manufacturing. The two main types of manufacturing are food processing and meat packing. Other important manufacturing businesses are textiles, cement, petroleum, chemicals, iron, steel, automobiles, and machinery.

This country is one of the world's top producers of wheat, rye, maize (corn), and linseed. The amount of livestock produced is among the highest in the world. Approximately 60% of the land here is used for agriculture.

The people of this South American country enjoy many leisure activities. Soccer is the most popular sport. Pato is also a favorite sport. It is played on horseback with a six-handled ball. The tango, a very popular dance, was invented here. It is especially popular during celebrations, such as Carnival. The national drink, mate, is sipped through a straw from a gourd and is made by brewing dried leaves of the native holly tree.

Where in the world are you?

Political Map of Argentina

Directions: Use the map of Argentina to answer the questions. Circle the correct answers.

1. San Juan is approximately _____ kilometers from Córdoba.
   - a. 400
   - b. 300
   - c. 100
   - d. 600

2. All of these cities except _____ are located along the Rio Paraná.
   - a. Santa Fe
   - b. Resario
   - c. Córdoba
   - d. Buenos Aires

3. The southernmost city in Argentina is _____.
   - a. Comodoro Rivadavia
   - b. Resistencia
   - c. Puerto Santa Cruz
   - d. Ushuaia

4. The city of _____ is located on the Atlantic Coast.
   - a. San Juan
   - b. Bahia Blanca
   - c. Rio Cuarto
   - d. Córdoba

5. The city located closest to the border of Chile is _____.
   - a. San Juan
   - b. Resistencia
   - c. Buenos Aires
   - d. Bahia Blanca

6. Patagonia is further _____ than the Pampas.
   - a. north
   - b. east
   - c. south
   - d. west

7. Rio Cuarto is about _____ miles from the Rio Paraná.
   - a. 200
   - b. 300
   - c. 400
   - d. 500

Argentina

- ---- International Boundary
- ★ National Capital
- • Major Cities
- — Rivers

0 100 200 300 Kilometers

0 100 200 300 Miles

CD-4347 • World Geography

Argentina Word Find

Directions: Find and circle the hidden words in the puzzle below.

```
C P S A P M F I E B R K H F J N V Z U O
A R A P D A O O B M R X U E S B D M H R
C O B M A E T U O F X O U D G Q U P A Q
K M U P P N C A N H J Z J O V K N S I Q
Q A E F P A I I G T H C C F O A U P P T
A N N W F X G S L O A Y D Y G J R X A P
D C O J V C A U H B N C E M Y G N N A P
G A S X X T S K M Q U I O E C R G N A E
N T A K A G E G B I V P A N K O D T J I
I H I A Z O B H D P H H E B C E O K E T
R O R I G T F O D V I B T R S A N W S C
U L E M K O O F U V W E F M O C G O L L
T I S A F Q O D D A L Y O C A C C U X O
C C L T T S S B H Z N U A R O C M M A X
A E M O C V A Y F L N H N R E S P A O P
F C R P V S G Z T T C I D R P A V E T W
U U M O Q E D S A N V O B L Q T D V S E
N C Z S M G W I A A B K Y J G K C D I O
A Z R E U W N R L A F V M F I X R E T B
M A B M K S G X Y X I T F A B S R O O E
```

ANDES MOUNTAINS   MANUFACTURING   ROMAN CATHOLIC

BUENOS AIRES   PAMPA   MESOPOTAMIA

CARNIVAL   REPUBLIC   PATO

CÓRDOBA   TANGO   SOCCER

PESO   MATE   GRAN CHACO

SPANISH   PATAGONIA   MOUNT ACONCAGUA

Where in the World Are You?

Capital: Santiago
Largest Cities: Santiago, Valparaiso, Viña del Mar
Population: 15,665,216 (July 2003 est.)
Land Area: 289,113 sq. mi. (748,800 sq km)
Highest Mountain: Nevado Ojos del Salado (22,572 ft./6,880 m)
Main Language: Spanish
Ethnic Groups: White, Amerindian
Main Religion: Roman Catholic
Government: Republic
Basic Currency: Peso

The flag has two horizontal stripes of white and red with a blue square in the upper left side that contains a five-pointed star.

You have arrived in a country whose name means "deepest point of the earth." The land stretches from the border with Peru to the southern tip of the continent at Cape Horn, and includes the largest part of Tierra del Fuego, an archipelago that is separated from the mainland by the Strait of Magellan. The average width of this country is 110 mi. (177 km) and the length is more than 2,610 mi. (4,200 km). The country is a bit larger than the state of Texas in land area.

There are three main land regions, including the Andes Mountains, the Central Valley, and a coastal escarpment. The Andes separate the country from Argentina and Bolivia. They include the volcanoes Maipu and Ojos del Salado, the second highest mountain in the Western Hemisphere. The Central Valley contains several fertile river basins. The escarpment is about 2,500 ft. (762 m) high and ends in steep cliffs along the Pacific Coast.

The Atacama Desert located in northern Chile is the second driest place in the world. The desert is located in the rain shadow of the Andes Mountains. Some places in the desert, such as Calama, have never received any measurable amounts of precipitation. Much of the country's mineral resources are mined in this region. Mining provides about half of the country's exports and employs about 2% of the working population. Copper is the leading mineral export and comes from the desert area. Iron ore, coal, sodium nitrate, iodine, borax, molybdenum, gold, silver, lead, and zinc are also mined in large amounts in the country.

Most people live in cities with both modern skyscrapers and traditional Spanish-style buildings. The cities also have plazas or public squares, parks, and gardens. Most people dress in Western style clothing. For special occasions, some cowboys, called huasos, wear colorful sashes, ponchos, big hats with flat tops, boots, spurs, and leggings with fringe. Like in other South American countries, the favorite sport here is soccer. Performances such as movies, plays, and concerts are popular with people who live in cities. Many wealthier people enjoy skiing. Those who live in rural areas enjoy visits with friends and neighbors and family outings.

The main foods are beans, potatoes, and bread. Cazuela de ave is a traditional type of soup that is made with rice, vegetables, and chicken. Most people also enjoy meat and fish on a regular basis.

Where in the world are you?

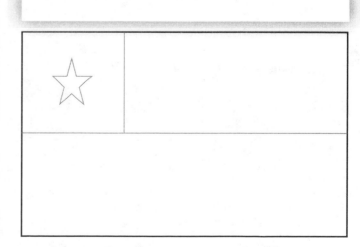

Political Map of Chile

Directions: Use the map of Chile to answer the questions. Circle the correct answers.

1. The capital of Chile is _____.
   a. Rancagua   b. Arica
   c. Santiago   d. Valparaiso

2. The southernmost city on this map of Chile is _____.
   a. Santiago   b. Punta Arenas
   c. Puerto Montt d. Arica

3. Rancagua is almost directly south of _____.
   a. Coquimbo   b. San Antonio
   c. Temuco   d. Santiago

4. The Atacama Desert is located to the _____ of Santiago.
   a. north   b. east
   c. south   d. west

5. Chile borders all of the following countries except _____.
   a. Paraguay   b. Peru
   c. Argentina   d. Bolivia

6. The distance from Temuco to Puerto Montt is about _____.
   a. 200 kilometers b. 200 miles
   c. 400 miles   d. 400 kilometers

7. All of these cities are along the Pacific Coast except _____.
   a. Concepción   b. Valparaiso
   c. Rancagua   d. Iquique

8. Of the following cities, the farthest from the Atacama Desert is _____.
   a. Punta Arenas b. San Antonio
   c. Puerto Montt d. Temuco

Graphs of People and Economy in Chile

Directions: Study the graphs and answer the questions. Circle the correct answers.

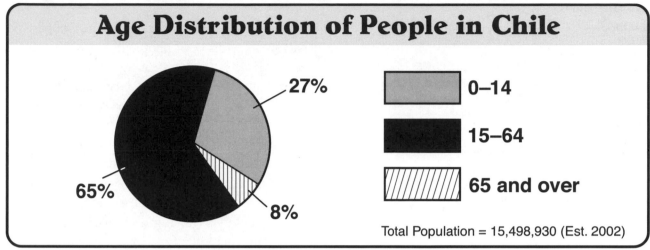

Age Distribution of People in Chile

27%

0–14

15–64

65 and over

65%

8%

Total Population = 15,498,930 (Est. 2002)

1. Most people in Chile are between the ages of _____ and _____.
   - a. 0 and 14
   - b. 15 and 64
   - c. 65 and over
   - d. 10 and 27

2. The percentage of people between 0 and 64 years of age is approximately _____.
   - a. 92
   - b. 100
   - c. 35
   - d. 73

3. The number of people between the ages of 0 and 14 is approximately _____.
   - a. 4,185,000
   - b. 1,240,000
   - c. 7,749,000
   - d. 15,499,000

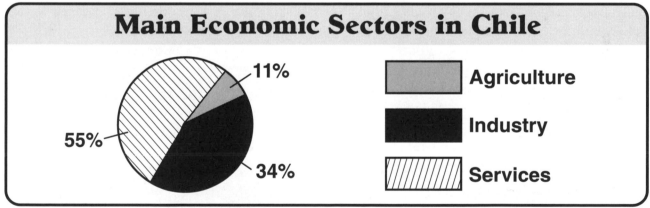

Main Economic Sectors in Chile

11%

Agriculture

Industry

Services

55%

34%

4. The total of the agricultural and industrial sectors equals _____.
   - a. 89%
   - b. 11%
   - c. 34%
   - d. 45%

5. More than half of the economy is supported by the _____ sector.
   - a. agriculture
   - b. industry
   - c. services
   - d. mining

6. Services produce approximately _____ times as much as agriculture.
   - a. two
   - b. four
   - c. five
   - d. ten

Where in the World Are You?

Capital: Brasilia
Largest Cities: São Paulo, Rio de Janeiro, and Salvador
Population: 182,032,604 (July 2003 est.)
Land Area: 3,265,081 sq. mi. (8,456,510 sq km)
Highest Mountain: Pico da Neblina (9,888 ft./ 3,014 m)
Main Languages: Portuguese, Spanish, English, French
Ethnic Groups: White, black, mixed Asian
Main Religion: Roman Catholic
Government: Federative republic
Basic Currency: Real

The flag consists of a green background with a large yellow diamond in the center that contains a blue circle with a white banner containing the motto, "Order and Progress."

Here you are in the largest country in South America. It is the fifth largest country in the world in both area and population. Low mountains and broad plateaus make up about two-thirds of this country. Forested lowlands complete the rest of the land area. The land stretches about 2,700 mi. (4,350 km) from the Andes Mountains to the Atlantic Ocean. There are four main landform regions including the Guiana Highlands, the Amazon River Basin, the Brazilian Highlands, and the Chaco. The Amazon River Basin has both tropical rain forests and jungle covered lowlands. The abundant wildlife found here includes the parrot, capybara, tapir, and monkey. The Amazon River is home to the flesh-eating piranha fish.

Coffee and sugar are two of the biggest crops exported from this country. Soybeans are produced and exported in large amounts. Other important commercial crops are cacao, tobacco, bananas, sugarcane, maize (corn), and oranges. More cattle are raised here than in Argentina. The country is the largest exporter of lumber in all of Latin America.

This has caused some environmentalists to protest the cutting of so many trees.

Approximately three-fourths of the people live in urban areas. Most poor people live in slums called favelas and have no sewer systems or running water. People in rural areas work on large plantations or ranches. Poor people in rural and urban areas eat mainly beans, rice, and manioc, a starchy root. City dwellers eat a variety of meats and wheat bread. One traditional dish is a stew made with pork and black beans, called feijoada. Most people speak the same language and practice the same religion. The official language is Portuguese, making this the largest Portuguese-speaking country in the world. Over 90% of the people practice the Roman Catholic religion; however, many people practice a variety of folk religions that combine Catholic and African themes.

Four days before Lent, the celebration of Carnival takes place. This is a spectacular folk festival and is a time when the country's most characteristic dance, the Samba, is featured. There are parades, singing, and dancing during this time. The parades feature colorful and elaborate costumes.

Where in the world are you?

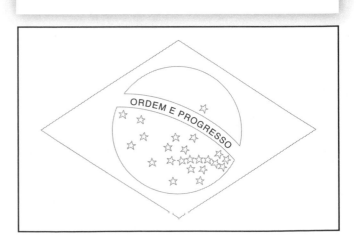

Political Map of Brazil

Directions: Use the map of Brazil to answer the questions. Circle the correct answers.

1. The Rio _____ forms part of the border between Brazil and Paraguay.
    a. Paraná   b. Amazon   c. Xingu   d. San Francisco

2. The city of _____ is not located along the Atlantic Coast of Brazil.
    a. Salvador   b. Brasilia   c. Recife   d. Rio de Janeiro

3. Each of these countries border Brazil except _____.
    a. Argentina   b. Guyana   c. Venezuela   d. Chile

4. The distance between Porto Velho and Rio Branco is approximately _____.
    a. 600 kilometers   b. 400 miles   c. 200 kilometers   d. 400 kilometers

5. The capital of Brazil is the city of _____.
    a. Rio de Janeiro   b. Brasilia   c. Rio Horizonte   d. Salvador

Deforestation

Deforestation is the cutting down, burning, and damaging of forests. In Brazil, this refers to the tropical rain forest called the Amazon. Deforestation happens for a variety of reasons. Forests are cut for agricultural purposes such as planting crops or grazing cattle, as well as for commercial logging. The problems resulting from deforestation include an increase in global warming, the loss or extinction of many species of plants and animals, and an increase in the greenhouse effect. The government of Brazil has used several successful programs to preserve the remaining rain forests. Many people are still concerned over the continued destruction of the Amazon rain forest.

Directions: Use the chart below to answer the following questions.

Rate of Deforestation in Brazil		
Years	**Square Miles**	**Square Kilometers**
1989-1990	5,332	13,810
1990-1991	4,297	11,130
1991-1992	5,323	13,786
1992-1994	5,571	14,896
1994-1995	11,219	29,059
1995-1996	7,012	18,161
1996-1997	5,107	13,227
1997-1998	6,712	17,383

1. The smallest amount of deforestation took place between _____.
   a. 1996-1997   b. 1989-1990   c. 1994-1995   d. 1990-1991

2. More deforestation took place between 1992 and 1994 than between _____.
   a. 1995-1996   b. 1991-1992   c. 1994-1995   d. 1997-1998

3. How many more square miles of deforestation were there between 1994-1995 than between 1995-1996?
   a. 4,207   b. 4,007   c. 3,107   d. 18,231

4. Between 1989 and 1991, what was the decrease in square kilometers of deforestation?
   a. 4,680   b. 2,680   c. 24,940   d. 4,933

Where in the World Are You?

Capital: Lima
Largest Cities: Lima, Arequipa, and Callao
Population: 28,409,897 (July 2003 est.)
Land Area: 494,211 sq. mi. (1,280,000 sq km)
Highest Mountain: Nevado Huascarán (22,205 ft./6,768 m)
Main Languages: Spanish, Quechua, Aymara
Ethnic Groups: Amerindian, Mestizo
Main Religion: Roman Catholic
Government: Constitutional republic
Basic Currency: Nuevo sol

The flag has three vertical stripes of red, white, and red with the coat of arms centered on the white stripe.

Here you are in the third largest country in South America. From north to south, it measures 1,225 mi. (1,971 km) and from east to west, it measures 875 mi. (1,408 km). The coastline measures 1,448 mi. (2,330 km). The highest navigable lake in the world, Lake Titicaca, is located on the border with Bolivia. The lake is 12,507 ft./3,812 m above sea level. There are three main land regions. One is an arid coastal plain, which varies in width from 10 to 100 miles (16-160 km) and contains most of the population. This is made possible because of the use of irrigation from the many streams that pass through the region. A second land region is the Andes Mountains which cover about 27% of the land. This highland area is well-watered and stretches from the border of Ecuador along the entire length of the country. The third region is part of the Amazon River basin, and it covers about 56% of the land. Here you can find tropical forests and jungles.

The country has several economic problems caused by an unstable government. The main occupation is farming. The major crops include bananas, coffee, cotton, potatoes, and sugar cane. The leading exports are coffee, copper, cotton, fish meal, petroleum, sugar, and silver.

Approximately 45% of the people who live in this country are descendents of the Incas. The walled city of Machu Picchu is a ruin of the ancient Incans. The highland Indians live at elevations of up to 15,000 ft. (4,570 m) above sea level.

Food is purchased daily at local markets or small stores. One of the basic foods is corn. The main diet of the people includes beans, rice, fish, and tropical fruit. The main ingredients in many dishes are rice, chicken, potatoes, pork, lamb, and fish. There are about 200 varieties of potatoes grown in the area of Lake Titicaca. The potatoes come in a variety of colors including blue, purple, yellow, and brown. A hot pepper, called aji, is also used quite often. Ceviche is a traditional food made of raw fish marinated in lemon juice and olive oil. Another traditional dish is anticuchos, which is marinated beef hearts.

The Aymara people enjoy music and dance. Musicians in this country play a flute made of varying lengths of bamboo, the siqu, pan pipes made of two rows of bamboo canes and ocarinas, oval-shaped clay with holes. They also use rattles called shaishas, made of polished goat hooves, which are tied together.

Where in the world are you?

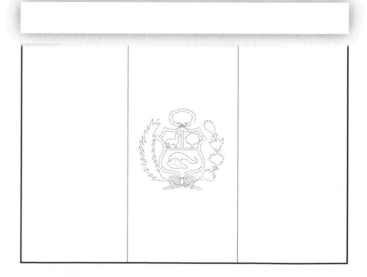

Political Map of Peru

Directions: Use the map of Peru to answer the questions. Circle the correct answers.

1. The capital city of _____ is located along the Pacific Coast.
   a. Callao   b. Matarani
   c. Chimbote   d. Lima

2. The distance between Cusco and Puerto Maldonado is about _____
   a. 200 mi.   b. 250 mi.
   c. 200 km   d. 250 km

3. The city of _____ is located along the Rio Ucayali.
   a. Huancayo
   b. Pucallpa
   c. Huánuco
   d. Puerto Maldonado

4. It is approximately _____ from Salaverry to Huánuco.
   a. 200 mi.   b. 400 mi.
   c. 200 km   d. 400 km

5. The city of _____ is located along the Pacific Coast of Peru.
   a. Puerto Maldonado   b. Matarani
   c. Yurimaguas   d. Pucallpa

Peru Crossword Puzzle

Directions: Complete the puzzle using the clues shown below.

Across

1. Pan pipes made of varying lengths of bamboo
3. Highest navigable lake in the world
6. Traditional dish of raw fish marinated in lemon juice and olive oil
7. Highest mountain in Peru
11. A basic food of the Peruvian people

Down

1. Main language of Peru
2. A walled ancient Incan city
4. Peruvian pepper
5. Rattles made of goat hooves
8. Native people who enjoy music and dance
9. Mountains found in Peru
10. Type of Peruvian currency

South America Time Line

Directions: Use the time line to answer the questions.

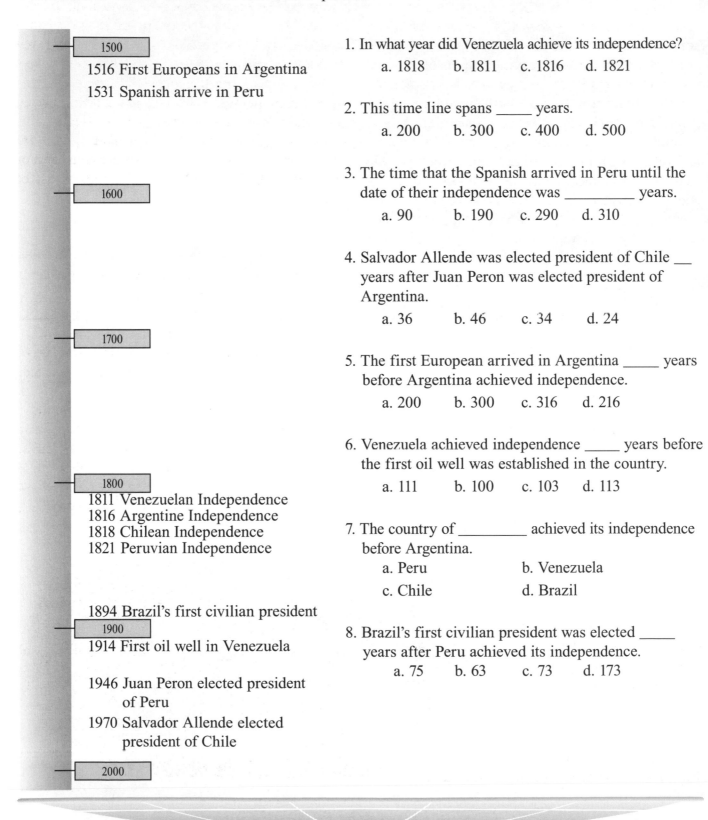

1500

1516 First Europeans in Argentina
1531 Spanish arrive in Peru

1600

1700

1800
1811 Venezuelan Independence
1816 Argentine Independence
1818 Chilean Independence
1821 Peruvian Independence

1894 Brazil's first civilian president
1900
1914 First oil well in Venezuela

1946 Juan Peron elected president
of Peru
1970 Salvador Allende elected
president of Chile

2000

1. In what year did Venezuela achieve its independence?
   a. 1818   b. 1811   c. 1816   d. 1821

2. This time line spans _____ years.
   a. 200   b. 300   c. 400   d. 500

3. The time that the Spanish arrived in Peru until the date of their independence was _____ years.
   a. 90   b. 190   c. 290   d. 310

4. Salvador Allende was elected president of Chile __ years after Juan Peron was elected president of Argentina.
   a. 36   b. 46   c. 34   d. 24

5. The first European arrived in Argentina _____ years before Argentina achieved independence.
   a. 200   b. 300   c. 316   d. 216

6. Venezuela achieved independence _____ years before the first oil well was established in the country.
   a. 111   b. 100   c. 103   d. 113

7. The country of _____ achieved its independence before Argentina.
   a. Peru   b. Venezuela
   c. Chile   d. Brazil

8. Brazil's first civilian president was elected _____ years after Peru achieved its independence.
   a. 75   b. 63   c. 73   d. 173

Physical Geography of Australia & Oceania

Location:

Australia and most of Oceania are located in the eastern hemisphere. Some of the islands, including the Hawaiian Islands, are located in the western hemisphere. To the west and south of Australia is the Indian Ocean and to the north and east is the Pacific Ocean. The Pacific Islands, known as Oceania, are found in the Pacific Ocean. These islands are located to the east of Japan, Indonesia, and the Philippines and to the west of North and South America. One island, New Guinea, is divided between two countries and two geographic regions. The eastern portion of the island of New Guinea forms the independent nation of Papua New Guinea and is considered part of Oceania. The western portion of the island, Irian Jaya, is a province of Indonesia and is considered part of Southeast Asia.

Area:

Australia is about 3,000,000 sq. mi. (7,500,000 sq km) in area. By combining all of the Pacific Islands, their land area would measure approximately 320,000 sq. mi. (820,000 sq km). In comparison, the area of the United States is still about 200,000 sq. mi. (520,000 sq km) larger than the total area of Australia and the Pacific Islands. If you measured the greatest distance in Australia from north to south, it would be 1,950 miles (3,138 km) and 2,475 miles (3,983 km) from east to west. From north to south, the measurement from Midway, Oceania to the South Island, New Zealand is approximately 5,000 miles (8,000 km). Mount Kosciusko, the highest point (7,310 ft./2,228 m), is in Australia. The lowest point, also in Australia, is Lake Eyre (52 ft./16 m below sea level).

Landforms:

There are three main landforms in Australia: desert, grassland, and highlands. Deserts and grasslands are main features of western Australia. Here you will find flat land with few trees. Large, dry grasslands border the deserts. Running the entire length of eastern Australia are the highlands. Included in this area are numerous plateaus, low mountains, and ranges of hills. Coastal plains are located between the highlands and the Pacific Ocean. Oceania is comprised of islands. This region consists of two main types of islands, high and low. The high islands, many of which contain volcanoes, are mountainous and/or hilly. Coral reefs created the low islands, most of which are atolls.

Climate:

The climate in most of this region is warm year-round. This is due to the location of many islands within the tropics. The precipitation in this area varies from a few inches (cm) to about 150 inches (380 cm) in a year. Northern Australia lies within the tropics; however, the southern two-thirds of the area does not. The southern region experiences warm to hot summers. In general, the majority of Australia receives less than 20 inches (51 cm) of rain yearly. On the other hand, New Zealand's climate is cooler and wetter. Because this region lies below the equator, its seasons are the opposite of those in Europe and North America. January and February are summer months while July and August are winter months.

Physical Map of Australia and Melanesia

Directions: Using an atlas or map of Oceania, identify by letter the following Pacific Islands on the map below.

_____ 1. Great Barrier Reef   _____ 6. Tasman Sea   _____ 11. Soloman Islands

_____ 2. New Zealand   _____ 7. Papua New Guinea   _____ 12. Indian Ocean

_____ 3. Greater Victoria Desert   _____ 8. Great Dividing Range   _____ 13. Kimberley Plateau

_____ 4. Fiji   _____ 9. New Caledonia   _____ 14. Tasmania

_____ 5. Pacific Ocean   _____ 10. Coral Sea   _____ 15. Gulf of Carpentaria

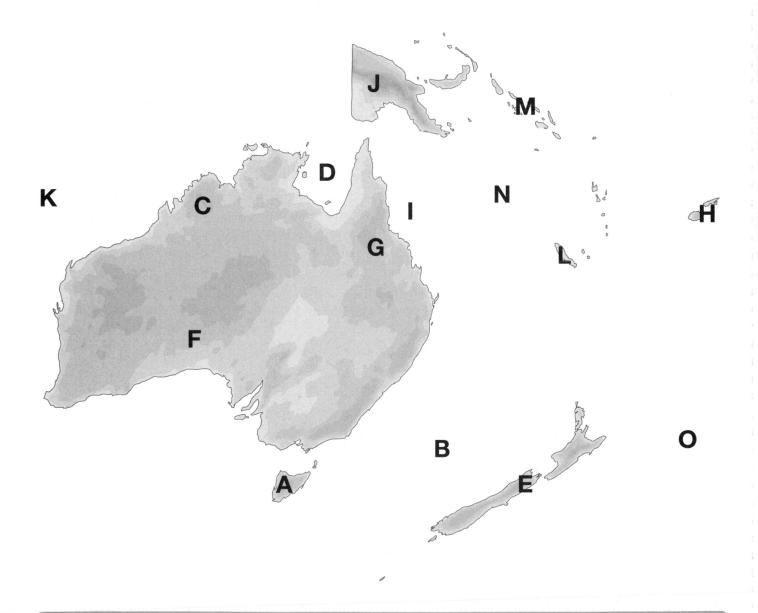

Where in the World Are You?

Capital: Canberra
Location: Between the South Pacific and Indian Oceans
Largest Cities: Sydney, Melbourne, and Brisbane
Population: 19,731,984 (July 2003 est.)
Land Area: 2,941,301 sq. mi. (7,617,930 sq km)
Highest Mountain: Mount Kosciusko (7,313 ft./ 2,229 m)
Main Language: English
Ethnic Groups: Caucasian, Asian, Aboriginal
Main Religion: Anglican, Roman Catholic
Government: Constitutional Monarchy
Basic Currency: Dollar

The flag consists of a blue field with the United Kingdom's flag in the upper hoist-side quadrant, below which is centered a large seven-pointed white star representing the country's states and territories. Five white stars, representing the constellation Southern Cross, are centered on the flag's outer half.

The next stop on a tour of the world is a dry, thinly-populated land. Only a few areas along or near the coasts receive enough rainfall to support a large population. By far, most people live in the southeastern coastal region. The two largest cities—Sydney and Melbourne—lie in this region. Canberra, the national capital, lies only a short distance inland. The huge interior of this country is mostly desert or dry grassland and has few settlements. The country as a whole averages only six people per square mile (two people per square kilometer). It is famous for its vast open spaces, bright sunshine, enormous numbers of sheep and cattle, and unusual wildlife. Kangaroos, koalas, platypuses, and wombats are only a few of the unusual animals that live in this country.

The first inhabitants were people known today as Aborigines who had lived on the continent for 65,000 years before the first white settlers arrived.

The United Kingdom settled there in 1788 and used the island as a prison colony. Since then, the number of whites has steadily increased, and the number of Aborigines has declined. Today, the majority of the people in this country are white.

The country is comprised of six states—New South Wales, Queensland, Tasmania, Victoria, South Australia, and Western Australia—and two territories—the Capital Territory and the Northern Territory. Each territory is responsible for its own administration. The country has three main land regions: the Eastern Highlands, the Central Lowlands, and the Western Plateau.

Family life is very similar to that of the North American family. Since much of the population came from Great Britain, there are British influences in much of the culture. Because meat is in abundant supply, it plays an important part in their diet. A typical dinner consists of meat, potatoes, and a second vegetable. Education varies, depending on the state or territory. In most areas, children attend from the age of five to fifteen. Most children attend free public school. Children who live in the Outback (rural interior of the country) study at home and are instructed by a teacher who talks to them via a two-way radio.

Where in the world are you?

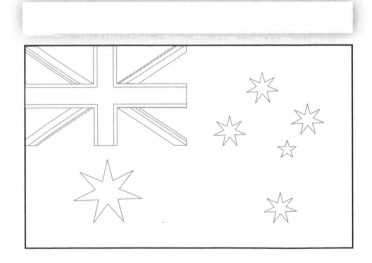

Political Map of Australia

Directions: Use the map of Australia to answer the questions. Circle the correct answers or fill in the blanks.

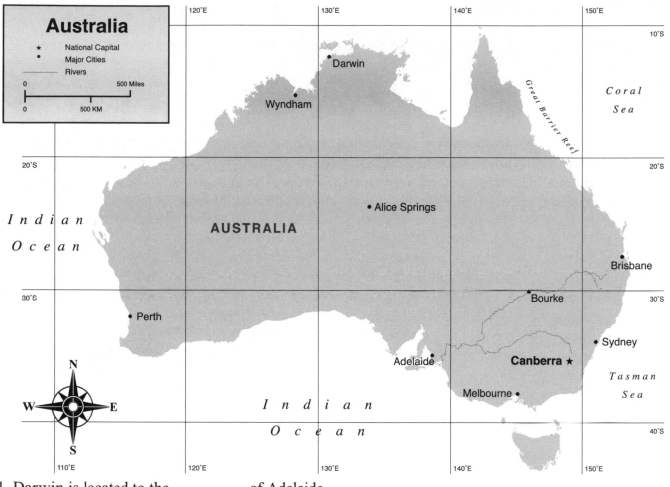

1. Darwin is located to the _____ of Adelaide.
   a. northeast   b. northwest   c. southeast   d. southwest

2. The distance between Bourke and Brisbane is almost _____ miles.
   a. 1,000   b. 2,000   c. 500   d. 250

3. _____ is located at 134° E longitude and 24° S latitude.

4. What city is located at 37° S and 145° E? _____

5. What physical feature is located off the northeast coast of Australia? _____

6. What city is located at approximately 32° S latitude and 116° E longitude? _____

7. _____ is located at 128° E longitude and 15° S latitude.

How to Make a Boomerang

How to Make a Boomerang

A boomerang, commonly associated with the Aborigines, the native people of Australia, is a curved, flat implement that is thrown as a weapon or for sport. Most boomerangs measure from 12 to 36 inches (30 to 90 centimeters) long and ½ to 5 inches (1.3 to 13 centimeters) wide. Their weight usually ranges from 1 to 18 ounces (30 to 500 grams). Most boomerangs have a bend, called the elbow, near the middle that forms two wings. Some boomerangs used for sport typically have two, three, or four wings.

There are two kinds of boomerangs, returning and nonreturning. Returning boomerangs are the best-known. When a returning boomerang is thrown correctly, the thrower can catch it without moving from the starting point. Different designs of returning boomerangs are made for right- and left-handed throwers. Nonreturning boomerangs are useful weapons for hunting and fighting.

Materials

1 piece of sturdy cardboard
1 bottle of school glue
1 roll of 1-inch masking tape
1 pair of scissors or craft knife
1 boomerang pattern

Directions

1. Enlarge the pattern to 17″ x 24″. Cut out the base of the boomerang using the outer edge of the pattern.
2. Then modify the pattern by trimming the pattern edge to the inner line. Using the smaller pattern, cut a second piece to fit on top of the base.
3. Place the smaller boomerang shape on top of the base in the center, leaving a ¼″ around the base on all sides. Use glue to place the top piece. Add small pieces of masking tape to secure the boomerang layers.
4. Tape the edges lengthwise with masking tape, smoothing out all ridges. Repeat the process on the curved ends. The entire boomerang can be covered with masking tape and painted, if desired.
5. Always throw the boomerang in an open area, usually outdoors.

Capital: Wellington
Largest Cities: Auckland, Wellington, and Christchurch
Population: 3,951307 (July 2003 est.)
Land Area: 103,738 sq. mi. (268,680 sq km)
Highest Mountain: Mount Cook (12,349 ft./3,764 m)
Main Languages: English, Maori
Ethnic Groups: European, Maori
Main Religion: Anglican, Presbyterian, Roman Catholic
Government: Parliamentary democracy
Basic Currency: Dollar

The flag consists of a blue shield with the United Kingdom's flag in the upper hoist-side quadrant. Four white-trimmed red stars on the flag's outer half represent the constellation Southern Cross.

This island country in the Southwest Pacific Ocean lies about 1,000 miles (1,600 kilometers) southeast of Australia and about 6,500 miles (10,500 kilometers) southwest of California. The country belongs to a large island group called Polynesia. The country consists of two main islands—the North Island and the South Island—and several dozen much smaller islands. Most of the smaller islands are several hours by boat from the main islands. Wellington is the capital city, while Auckland is the largest city. The country was once part of the British Empire. Today, it is an independent member of the Commonwealth of Nations, an association of countries that replaced the empire.

The island is a beautiful country of snow-capped mountains, green lowlands, beaches, and many lakes and waterfalls. No place is more than 80 miles (130 kilometers) from the coast, and in few places are mountains or hills out of view. Overall, the country has a mild, moist climate. Since it is south of the equator, its seasons are opposite those of the Northern Hemisphere. July is the coldest month and January is the warmest.

A people called the Maori were the first to live here. They came from Polynesian islands located northeast of this island. Europeans discovered the country in 1642, but they did not settle on the islands until the late 1700's.

The standard of living ranks among the highest in the world. For many years, the country's economy depended largely on agriculture. Today, agriculture, manufacturing, and service industries are all important to the economy. The sale of butter, cheese, meat, and wool to other countries provides much of the nation's income.

The people of this country love outdoor activities and sports. Many city families own baches (cabins) in resort areas, where they go on weekends. The nation's mild climate the year round makes camping, hiking, hunting, and mountain climbing possible in any season. Many people enjoy cricket, which somewhat resembles baseball, and rugby, a form of football.

The people are perhaps the best-fed in the world. They eat more butter and meat per person than any other people. Lamb is the favorite meat. Kumaras (sweet potatoes) may accompany lamb and other meat dishes. A special treat is toheroa soup, made from a native green clam. Tea is the favorite drink.

Where in the world are you?

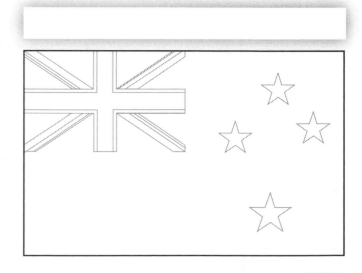

Political Map of New Zealand

Directions: Use the map of New Zealand to answer the questions. Circle the correct answers.

1. On which island is the city of Christchurch located?
   - a. South Island
   - b. North Island
   - c. Stewart Island
   - d. Australia

2. What waterway lies between the North and South Islands?
   - a. Tasman Sea
   - b. Cook Strait
   - c. Pacific Ocean
   - d. Pegasus Bay

3. The distance between Napier and Wellington is at least _____.
   - a. 75 kilometers
   - b. 150 kilometers
   - c. 150 miles
   - d. 75 miles

4. Gisborne is _____ of Dunedin.
   - a. northeast
   - b. northwest
   - c. southwest
   - d. southeast

5. The capital of New Zealand is _____.
   - a. Auckland
   - b. Wellington
   - c. New Plymouth
   - d. Palmerston North

6. The distance between Greymouth and Christchurch is approximately
   - a. 150 kilometers
   - b. 150 miles
   - c. 75 kilometers
   - d. 300 kilometers

7. Auckland is almost directly north of _____.
   - a. Dargaville
   - b. Wellington
   - c. Gisborne
   - d. Invercargill

8. All of the following cities are located along the Tasman Sea coast except _____.
   - a. Greymouth
   - b. Napier
   - c. Auckland
   - d. New Plymouth

A Closer Look at New Zealand

Directions: Using pages 46 and 47, and a reference book, match the description in the first column with a place name in the second column.

_____ 1. the highest point in New Zealand

_____ 2. island of New Zealand belongs to this group

_____ 3. the national capital

_____ 4. body of water which lies to the east of New Zealand

_____ 5. first people to live in New Zealand

_____ 6. type of government in New Zealand

_____ 7. the largest city in New Zealand

_____ 8. the island at the southern tip of the South Island

_____ 9. Four white-trimmed red stars on the flag's outer half represent the _____.

_____ 10. an association of countries that replaced the British Empire

_____ 11. For many years, the country's economy depended largely on _____.

_____ 12. People of New Zealand enjoy this sport which resembles baseball.

A. Polynesia

B. Commonwealth of Nations

C. cricket

D. Maori

E. North Island

F. Stewart Island

G. South Pacific Ocean

H. agriculture

I. Constitutional monarchy

J. Southern Cross

K. Mount Cook

L. Auckland

M. rugby

N. Wellington

O. Tasman Sea

Where in the World Are You?

The Pacific Islands is the name given to a group of thousands of islands scattered across the Pacific Ocean. No one seems to know exactly how many islands are in the Pacific. Geographers estimate that there are from 20,000 to 30,000. Some islands cover thousands of square miles or square kilometers; however, others are no more than tiny piles of rock or sand that barely rise above the ocean.

Although some islands are large, all of them together cover less land than does the state of Alaska. New Guinea is the largest island in the group and the second largest island in the world, after Greenland. New Zealand's two main islands are the second and third largest islands. Together with New Guinea, they comprise more than four-fifths of the total land area of the Pacific Islands.

The islands can be divided into three main areas: Melanesia, Micronesia, and Polynesia. These areas are based on the geography of the islands and on the cultures and ethnic backgrounds of the native peoples.

Melanesia means black islands. Its name is derived from the word melanin, which is the pigment produced in the skin. The Melanesian people have large amounts of melanin in their skin, which makes their skin dark. Melanesia includes Papua New Guinea, the Solomon Islands, New Caledonia, and Vanuatu. Fiji is considered part of Melanesia because of its location; however, its culture is much more like that of Polynesia. The Melanesian islands lie south of the equator.

Micronesia means tiny islands. These islands lie north of Melanesia, and most of them also lie north of the equator. More than 2,000 islands make up Micronesia. Most of them are low-lying coral islands. Micronesia includes Guam, the Caroline Islands, the Mariana Islands, the Marshall Islands, the Gilbert Islands, and the single island of Nauru.

Polynesia, which means many islands, occupies the largest area in the South Pacific. There are long distances between its island groups. Polynesia stretches from Midway Island in the north to New Zealand, 5,000 miles (8,000 kilometers) to the south. The easternmost island in Polynesia, Easter Island, lies more than 4,000 miles (6,400 kilometers) from New Zealand.

The land and climate differ greatly throughout the islands. Many of the islands, especially those in Polynesia, are famous for sparkling white beaches, gentle ocean breezes, and swaying palm trees. Some other islands, especially in Melanesia, have thick jungles and tall mountain peaks. Many lowland areas are steaming hot, but the tallest mountain peaks are covered with snow throughout the year.

Almost 15 million people live in the Pacific Islands. Only a few islands or island groups, such as Fiji, Hawaii, New Guinea, and New Zealand, have large numbers of people. Many islands have fewer than a hundred people, and others have none at all. The first islanders came from Southeast Asia several thousand years ago. Their earliest settlements were in Melanesia and Micronesia. Most of Polynesia was settled later.

These groups of Pacific Islands comprise

Choose a country from this region and illustrate its flag in the box below.

Political Maps of Countries of Oceania

Directions: Use the maps below and page 49, or another reference source, to answer the questions. Circle the correct answers.

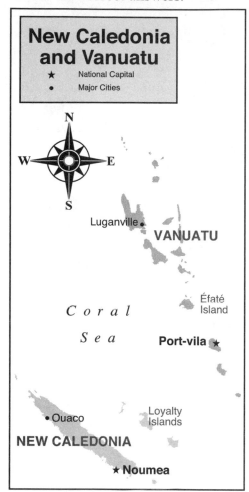

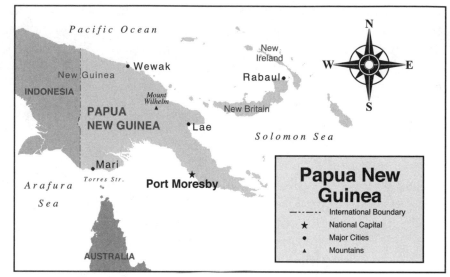

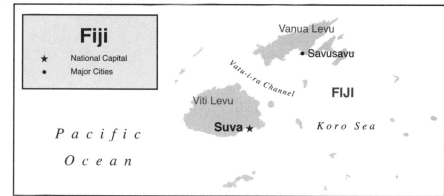

1. Mount Wilhelm is located in _____.
   - a. Vanuatu
   - b. Fiji
   - c. New Guinea
   - d. Papua New Guinea

2. The city of _____ is not located on the island of New Guinea.
   - a. Port Moresby
   - b. Lae
   - c. Rabaul
   - d. Mari

3. The islands named above are all part of the area called _____.
   - a. Melanesia
   - b. Micronesia
   - c. Hawaii
   - d. Polynesia

4. The two largest islands of Fiji are Vanua Levu and _____.
   - a. Viti Levu
   - b. Éfaté Island
   - c. New Britain
   - d. New Ireland

5. The body of water that separates the countries of New Caledonia and Vanuatu is _____.
   - a. Koro Sea
   - b. Coral Sea
   - c. Arafura Sea
   - d. Solomon Sea

Categorizing the Islands of Oceania

Directions: Using the information about the Pacific Islands found on page 49 as well as reference materials, place the following islands in their correct categories of Melanesia, Micronesia, and Polynesia.

Guam	Solomon Islands	New Caledonia
New Guinea	Fiji	Cook Islands
Gilbert Islands	Midway Island	Vanuatu
Hawaiian Islands	Easter Island	Marshall Islands
Mariana Islands	Caroline Islands	Marquesas Islands

Melanesia	Micronesia	Polynesia
_____	_____	_____
_____	_____	_____
_____	_____	_____
_____	_____	_____
_____	_____	_____

Searching the Pacific

Directions: Locate and circle the key words of Australia and the Pacific Islands listed below in the word find.

```
M J M F O A S K M O A T P Z N E R G V K
I M O T I C D U I J X Z E S G U U C U U
C D U H B J E S R R F F R E F A N M T L
R P N V X G I A O F O M U F M O A A M Y
O P T D U O N T N U S I O U R R U S U B
N P C T O E C U A I T R F T A N J O Z B
E L O K L S K I G B A H H S A A J T J P
S N O G U K K B S L M I E V T U K U A Q
I O K X G M I D G S S O A R Y S B A W L
A T M R B F U M M L D V W R N I M J F G
C G O W T D E D A N Z U H N R C Y L X Z
M N I M K O V N A L U W H X A E R G T O
H I U B H W D L X M K J F J U U B O I Z
S L M L N T S I Q X V S N P R I R N S C
E L A D Y I O M Q G A G T E Q K U A A S
Y E O B H I N D C H M M V G D O G W R C
D W G T R U U H B F G A I S E N Y L O P
N U U O M E L A N E S I A S J K Z N N M
R O A Q U E E N S L A N D A M D C N Y C
S M A B O R I G I N E S E N O O A A H C
```

ABORIGINES	MAORI	NORTH ISLAND	SOUTHERN CROSS
CANBERRA	MELANESIA	OCEANIA	SOUTH ISLAND
FIJI	MICRONESIA	POLYNESIA	VANUATU
GUAM	MOUNT COOK	QUEENSLAND	WELLINGTON
KUMARAS	NAURA	RUGBY	WOMBAT

Physical Geography of Europe

Location:

Europe is located in the Eastern Hemisphere. Found west of the continent of Asia and north of the continent of Africa, Europe is bordered by the Atlantic Ocean to the west, the Arctic Ocean to the north, the Ural Mountains to the east, and the Black and Mediterranean Seas to the south. The whole continent is located above the equator in the Northern Hemisphere.

Area:

Europe ranks sixth in area of the seven continents. The only continent that is smaller in area is Australia. The total area of Europe is 4,066,000 sq. mi. (10,532,000 sq km). This means that Europe is approximately 500,000 sq. mi. (1,300,000 sq km) larger than the United States. At its greatest north-south distance, the continent of Europe is about 3,000 miles (4,800 km) long. Its greatest distance from east to west is about 4,000 miles (6,400 km) wide. Mount Elbrus (18,481 ft./5,633 m) is the highest point on the European continent. The lowest point is on the shore of the Caspian Sea (92 ft./28 m) below sea level.

Landforms:

Peninsulas, mountains, plains, islands, and rivers are the main landforms of Europe. Some of the largest European peninsulas are the Iberian, Scandinavian, Apennine, and Balkan. From north central Europe to the Ural Mountains in Russia, there is a huge plain stretching across the continent. This northern European plain is a very fertile area with numerous farmlands providing much of Europe's food. Industrial development has been encouraged because of the numerous minerals found in the northern European plain. In the center of eastern Europe is the smaller Great Hungarian Plain.

Most of Europe's mountains are located to the north and south. Norway, Sweden, Iceland, and the northern United Kingdom are mountainous areas. The Pyrenees Mountains border a large plateau in the Iberian Peninsula. The Iberian Peninsula contains two countries, Spain and Portugal. Much of southeastern Europe is covered by the Carpathian Mountains and the mountains of the Balkan Peninsula. The Apennine Peninsula contains mountains which stretch southward from the Alps.

There are numerous useful and important rivers which flow across the European continent. Europe's longest river is the Volga which is located in eastern Europe. Europe's second longest river, the Danube River (1,770 mi./2,850 km) is twice as long as the Rhine River.

Climate:

Some areas of Europe get very cold while others become very hot; however, in general, the climate of Europe is considered mild. In the far north, winters are long and cold with cool, short summers. In the far south, winters are mild, and summers are usually hot and dry. One of the major influences on the European climate are the winds which blow across the continent from the Atlantic Ocean. These winds help keep the climate mild even near the Arctic Circle.

Physical Map of Europe

Directions: Match the letters on the physical map of Europe with the physical features listed below.

____ 1. Pyrenees Mountains

____ 2. Iberian Peninsula

____ 3. Ural Mountains

____ 4. Great Hungarian Plain

____ 5. Balkan Peninsula

____ 6. Apennine Peninsula

____ 7. Carpathian Mountains

____ 8. Caspian Sea

____ 9. North Sea

____ 10. Arctic Ocean

____ 11. Mediterranean Sea

____ 12. Black Sea

____ 13. Scandinavian Peninsula

____ 14. Atlantic Ocean

Where in the World Are You?

Capital: Stockholm

Largest Cities: Stockholm, Göteborg, and Malmö

Population: 8,878,085 (July 2003 est.)

Land Area: 158,663 sq. mi. (410,934 sq km)

Highest Mountain: Mount Kebnekaise (6,926 ft./ 2,111 m)

Main Languages: Swedish

Ethnic Groups: Swedish, Finnish, Sami

Main Religion: Lutheran

Government: Constitutional monarchy

Basic Currency: Krona

The flag consists of a blue field with a yellow cross that is shifted slightly to the hoist side.

Located on the continent of Europe between Norway and Finland, this country is a land of beautiful lakes, snow-capped mountains, swift rivers, and rocky offshore islands. It is one of Europe's largest countries in area; however, it is also one of Europe's most thinly-populated countries. Forests cover more than half of the country's land. Only about a tenth of the country is farmland. The northernmost part lies inside the Arctic Circle in a region called the Land of the Midnight Sun because for periods during the summer, the sun shines 24 hours a day.

The climate varies greatly between the southern and northern parts of the country. Southwesterly winds from the Atlantic Ocean give the southern part pleasant summers and mostly mild winters. In contrast, the northern part of the country has pleasant summers but cold winters. In the extreme south of the country, temperatures in January and February, the coldest months, average 32° F (0° C); however, in the far north, temperatures average about 10° F (-12° C) during these months.

The standard of living is one of the highest in the world. In fact, this country ranks among the leading European nations in the number of automobiles, telephones, and television sets it has in relation to its population. Abundant natural resources, such as vast forests and rich deposits of iron ore, helped change the country from a poor agricultural nation to an advanced industrial society. The iron and steel industry produces high-quality steel, which is used for such products as ball bearings, stainless steel goods for the home, precision tools, and watch springs. The country's important engineering products include machinery, aircraft, automobiles, and ships. Linkoping is the chief center of the country's aircraft industry. Göteborg and Stockholm have major automobile plants. Nearly half the automobiles produced domestically by Volvo and Saab are exported to the United States.

This country is famous for smorgasbord, an assortment of cold and hot foods placed on a large table for self-service. The people often eat the foods in a particular order. First, they eat cold fish dishes, including eels, herring, salmon, sardines, and shrimp. Next, they eat such cold meats as liver pate, smoked reindeer, sliced beef, and ham with vegetable salad. Next come small hot dishes, such as meatballs, omelets, sausages, or herring cooked in bread crumbs. Favorite desserts include cheese, fresh fruit, fruit salad, and pastries.

Where in the world are you?

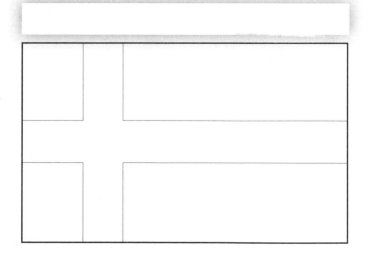

Political Map of Sweden

Directions: Use the map of Sweden to answer the questions. Circle the correct answers.

1. The capital of Sweden is _____.
   - a. Halmstad
   - b. Orebro
   - c. Umeå
   - d. Stockholm

2. The distance from Vasteras to Nykoping is approximately _____.
   - a. 100 miles
   - b. 200 miles
   - c. 50 kilometers
   - d. 100 kilometers

3. The body of water located between Sweden and Finland is _____.
   - a. Baltic Sea
   - b. Norwegian Sea
   - c. Gulf of Bothnia
   - d. North Sea

4. The country of _____ is located west of Sweden.
   - a. Norway
   - b. Finland
   - c. Latvia
   - d. Estonia

5. All of these cities are located along the Gulf of Bothnia except _____.
   - a. Umeå
   - b. Göteborg
   - c. Luleå
   - d. Gävle

6. The distance between Jokkmokk and Lulea is approximately _____.
   - a. 50 kilometers
   - b. 100 kilometers
   - c. 50 miles
   - d. 100 miles

7. Gävle is almost directly north of _____.
   - a. Örebro
   - b. Kiruna
   - c. Halmstad
   - d. Nykoping

8. _____ is closer to Finland than Norway.
   - a. Göteborg
   - b. Halmstad
   - c. Luleå
   - d. Karlstad

Sweden

- ----- International Boundary
- ★ National Capital
- • Major Cities

0 50 100 Kilometers

0 50 100 Miles

NORWAY

Kiruna •

Jokkmokk •

Norwegian Sea

• Luleå

Umeå •

FINLAND

NORWAY

SWEDEN

Gulf of Bothnia

• Gävle

• Uppsala

Gulf of Finland

Vasteras •

Karlstad •

★ Stockholm

Örebro •

ESTONIA

• Nykoping

Göteborg •

LATVIA

Halmstad •

Baltic Sea

LITHUANIA

DENMARK

Looking Closely at Sweden

Directions: Look closely at the statements about Sweden. Decide if the statements below are correct. Circle T if the statement is True and F if the statement is False.

T   F   1. Located in southern Europe, Sweden is situated between Norway and Finland.

T   F   2. Sweden's standard of living is one of the highest in the world.

T   F   3. In the Land of the Midnight Sun, the sun shines 24 hours a day during some periods of the summer.

T   F   4. Sweden's important engineering products include automobiles, asbestos, machinery, and ships.

T   F   5. Stockholm and Göteborg are considered the dual capitals of Sweden.

T   F   6. Linkoping is the chief center of the country's aircraft industry.

T   F   7. Vast forests and rich deposits of gold helped change Sweden from a poor agricultural nation to an advanced industrial society.

T   F   8. Nearly 90% of the automobiles (Volvo and Saab) made are exported to the United States.

T   F   9. Mount Kebnekaise (6,926 ft./2,111 m) is Sweden's highest mountain.

T   F   10. Sweden is famous for smorgasbord, an assortment of breads, cheese, and cold foods on a large table for self-service.

T   F   11. Sweden's form of government is a constitutional monarchy.

T   F   12. The flag consists of a blue field with a green cross that is shifted slightly to the hoist side.

Capital: Paris

Largest Cities: Paris, Marseille, Lyon, Toulouse, and Nice

Population: 60,180,529 (July 2003 est.)

Land Area: 210,669 sq. mi. (545,630 sq km)

Highest Mountain: Mount Blanc (15,771 ft./4,807 m)

Main Language: French

Ethnic Group: French

Main Religion: Roman Catholic

Government: Republic

Basic Currency: Euro

The flag consists of three equal vertical bands of blue, white, and red.

The third largest European country in area, this country shares borders with eight other countries. The snowcapped Alps in the southeastern part of the country form the border between this country and Italy. Sunny beaches and steep cliffs stretch along the southern coast on the Mediterranean Sea. Fishing villages dot the Atlantic coast of the northwestern part of the country. The peaceful, wooded Loire Valley of the central countryside has many historic chateaux (castles).

Paris, the capital and largest city, has been a world center of art and learning for hundreds of years. Every year, millions of tourists visit such famous Paris landmarks as the Cathedral of Notre Dame, the Eiffel Tower, and the Louvre—one of the largest art museums in the world.

Previous to World War II, the country's economy was primarily based on small farms and businesses. However, since the war, the country has worked to modernize production methods in order to be a major player in world economy and trade. It is, for example, one of the largest producers of automobiles in the world. This country also has large chemical and steel industries. It is a leader in growing wheat, grapes, potatoes, sugar beets, and apples.

Almost three-fourths of the people live in cities and towns. In the larger cities, most people live in apartments. The older a building is, the more prestigious it is, especially in Paris. These tenants are willing to live with outdated plumbing and other inconveniences in order to enjoy the decorative antique architecture. While city living is generally pleasant, it is more expensive.

Cyclists from around the world flock here every July to engage in the greatest national sporting event of this country. About 200 professional cyclists race for three weeks in the tour around this country and sometimes parts of neighboring countries. One of the most popular team sports is soccer. Most regions have their own teams. Boules, a form of bowling, is also enjoyed by many people. Tennis, swimming, ice skating, fishing, and basketball are also popular sports.

The people of this country feel that cooking is an art. Their gourmet cooking has set the standard for the rest of the world since the 1700's. Some of their specialties include bouillabaisse (a chunky chowder with fish and shellfish) and cassoulet (a casserole made with poultry, pork, sausage, and beans). Crusty bread is served with most meals.

Where in the world are you?

Political Map of France

Directions: Use the map of France to answer the questions. Circle the correct answers.

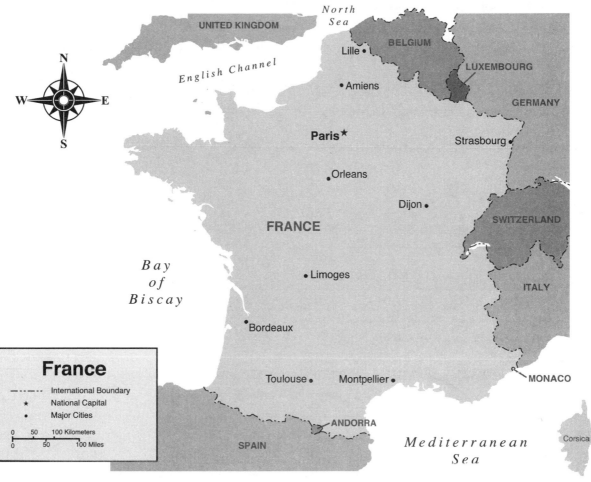

1. The body of water located to the south of France is _____.
   a. English Channel   b. Mediterranean Sea c. Atlantic Ocean   d. Bay of Biscay

2. The city of _____ is near the border of France and Belgium.
   a. Lille   b. Nancy   c. Toulouse   d. Dijon

3. The distance between Limoges and Montpellier is about _____.
   a. 100 miles   b. 100 kilometers   c. 200 miles   d. 200 kilometers

4. The country of _____ is located south of France.
   a. Germany   b. Italy   c. Spain   d. United Kingdom

5. The capital city of Paris is located _____ of Orleans.
   a. northeast   b. northwest   c. southeast   d. southwest

6. From the city of Bordeaux to Toulouse, it is approximately _____ kilometers.
   a. 25   b. 50   c. 100   d. 200

France Crossword Puzzle

Directions: Using the information on page 59 and other resources, complete the crossword puzzle using the clues shown below.

Across

2. Famous bicycle race in France
6. Capital city
7. Mountains between France and Italy
8. Type of French cooking
9. France has large _____ and steel industries.
11. Type of casserole made with meat and beans
12. Famous Parisian cathedral

Down

1. Form of bowling popular in France
3. Type of government
4. Where three-fourths of the people in France live
5. Beautiful buildings found in Loire Valley
10. One of the largest museums in the world

Where in the World Are You?

Capital: Vienna

Largest Cities: Vienna, Gratz, Linz, Salzburg, and Innsbruck

Population: 8,188,207 (July 2003 est.)

Land Area: 31,945 sq. mi. (83,738 sq km)

Highest Mountain: Grossglockner (12,460 ft./ 3,798 m)

Main Language: German

Ethnic Group: German

Main Religion: Roman Catholic

Government: Federal republic

Basic Currency: Euro

The flag consists of three horizontal stripes of red, white, and red with the coat of arms in the center of the white stripe.

This small, central European country is famous for its beautiful mountain scenery, covering three-fourths of the country. Being a landlocked country, it shares a border with the countries of Italy, Switzerland, Germany, Slovenia, Slovakia, Hungary, Czech Republic, and Liechtenstein. Stretching across the western, southern, and central parts of the country are the Alps and their foothills. Many lovely mirror-like lakes can be found here. From north to south, it measures 180 miles (290 km) and from east to west it measures 355 miles (571 km).

The economy is very prosperous because of its many natural resources. This country leads the world in the production of magnesite (a mineral used to make heat-resistant products) and graphite. Products manufactured include electrical equipment, processed foods, textiles, glass, cement, and furniture. Because the country is so mountainous, only 20% of the land can be used for growing crops; however, the farmers use modern machinery and farming methods to supply more than three-fourths of the food for the people.

Millions of tourists visit the country every year. This adds more than a billion dollars to the annual national income each year. Many winter vacationers, especially skiers, are attracted to Innsbruck, Kitzbuhel, and other sports centers in the Alps. The numerous art galleries, concert halls, and museums, especially in Vienna, also attract many tourists.

Children between the ages of 6 and 15 are required to attend school. In this country the literacy rate is 100% —all adults can read and write. Most students attend free public schools. Students can choose from a variety of educational programs.

More than half of the people live in cities and towns. Many city dwellers live in apartment buildings. In the rural areas, families live in one-family homes that vary in style from region to region. Many great composers have originated from this country, including Mozart, Haydn, Schubert, and Strauss.

A favorite dish of this country, wiener schnitzel (breaded veal cutlet), is popular in other European countries. Dumplings, noodles, or potatoes are included as side dishes in most meals. Holidays and festivals are important. One such festival is celebrated at the beginning of spring. During this time, people pretend to chase away the "evil spirits" of winter.

Where in the world are you?

Political Map of Austria

Directions: Use the map of Austria to answer the questions. Circle the correct answers.

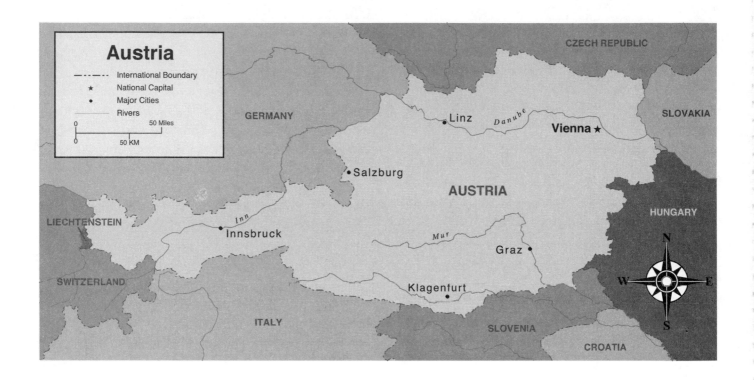

1. The capital city of Austria is _____.
   a. Salzburg   b. Innsbruck   c. Klagenfurt   d. Vienna

2. The city of _____ is located along the Danube River.
   a. Graz   b. Salzburg   c. Linz   d. Klagenfurt

3. The country of _____ borders Austria to the south.
   a. Germany   b. Slovenia   c. Czech Republic   d. Croatia

4. The distance between the cities of Salzburg and Linz is approximately _____.
   a. 100 kilometers   b. 100 miles   c. 200 miles   d. 50 kilometers

5. The city of _____ is located near the border of Austria and Germany.
   a. Vienna   b. Linz   c. Innsbruck   d. Salzburg

6. The city of _____ is farthest from Vienna.
   a. Linz   b. Graz   c. Klagenfurt   d. Salzburg

Exploring Austria

Directions: Complete the crossword puzzle using the clues below.

Across

1. The main language of Austria
3. Only 20% of the land is used for crops because Austria is so _____.
7. Popular dish of breaded veal cutlet
9. Tourism contributes more than one _____ dollars to the national income.
11. Type of currency used in Austria

Down

1. The highest mountain
2. One of the great musical composers from Austria
4. Mountains found in the western, southern, and central parts of Austria
5. The capital of Austria
6. Austria leads the world in the production of magnesite and _____.
8. Town visited by many skiers and winter vacationers
10. Boot-shaped country bordering Austria to the southwest

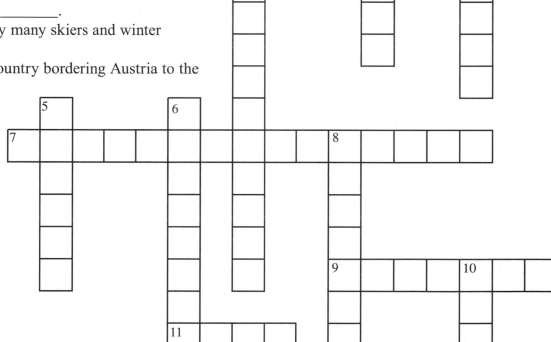

Where in the World Are You?

Capital: Rome
Largest Cities: Rome, Milan, Naples, and Turin
Population: 57,998,353 (July 2003 est.)
Land Area: 113,522 sq. mi. (294,020 sq km)
Highest Mountain: Mont Blanc de Courmayeur (15,577 ft./4,748 m)
Main Language: Italian
Ethnic Groups: Italian
Main Religion: Roman Catholic
Government: Republic
Basic Currency: Euro

The flag consists of three vertical stripes of green, white, and red.

This boot-shaped peninsula, situated in southern Europe, is known for its rich cultural heritage and natural beauty. Within the country's borders lie two independent states: Vatican City and the tiny Republic of San Marino. In addition to the states, this country also includes two large islands, Sicily and Sardinia.

The landscape of this country is dominated by two mountain ranges—the Alps and the Apennines. The Alps tower over the northernmost part. The Apennines form a backbone that runs nearly the entire length of the peninsula. Its cities have spectacular churches and large central plazas. The country boasts several world-famous cities. Rome, the capital and largest city, was the center of the Roman Empire 2,000 years ago. Florence was the home of many artists of the Renaissance, a period of great achievements in the arts. Venice, with its intricate canal system, attracts thousands of tourists from all over the world.

Most people live in urban areas. The largest cities—Rome, Milan, and Naples—have more than a million people. Life in the northern part differs in many ways from that in the southern part of the country. The north is richer, more urbanized, and more industrial than the south. Service industries, manufacturing and construction employ the most people in both areas. In all parts of the country, most people live in cities or towns. The people are strongly attached to their towns, neighborhoods, and families. Most people who live in urban areas reside in concrete apartment buildings. A few wealthy people live in single-family homes.

The people of this country take great pride in the quality of their cooking. They traditionally eat their main meal at midday. Large meals usually consist of a pasta course, followed by a main course of meat or fish. Sometimes a course of antipasto (appetizers) is served before the pasta. The antipasto may consist of a variety of cold meats and vegetables, such as salami, olives, and artichoke hearts. Another popular first-course dish is risotto, a rice dish with vegetables. The most popular meats are veal and pork. Cheeses are also important. Fresh fruit is a popular dessert. Traditionally, wine is served with every meal except breakfast.

Soccer is the most popular sport. Every major city has a professional soccer team. Basketball is also very popular, and some cities have more than one basketball team. Other popular sports include cycling, roller skating, and baseball.

Where in the world are you?

Political Map of Italy

Directions: Use the map of Italy to answer the questions. Circle the correct answers.

1. What famous city, known for its canals, is located on the Adriatic Sea?
   - a. Milan
   - b. Bologna
   - c. Venice
   - d. Naples

2. The city of Palermo is located on the island of _____.
   - a. Sicily
   - b. Corsica
   - c. Sardinia
   - d. Rome

3. The capital city of Italy is _____.
   - a. Venice
   - b. Rome
   - c. Naples
   - d. Florence

4. The distance between Rome and Naples is approximately _____.
   - a. 50 kilometers
   - b. 50 miles
   - c. 100 kilometers
   - d. 100 miles

5. Milan is located in the _____ part of Italy.
   - a. northern
   - b. southern
   - c. eastern
   - d. western

6. The independent republic of San Marino is located almost directly _____ of Rome.
   - a. north
   - b. south
   - c. east
   - d. west

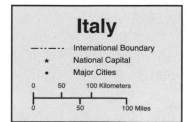

CD-4347 • World Geography

Famous Italian Recipes

Italian Sausage with Rice

Ingredients:
½ cup (120 mL) butter or margarine, divided
2 onions, coarsely chopped and divided
1 cup (240 mL) uncooked regular rice
4 cups (960 mL) boiling chicken broth
1 teaspoon (5 mL) salt
¼ teaspoon (1.25 mL) pepper
½ pound (227 g) Italian sausage, cut into 2-inch (5 cm) lengths
5 chicken livers (or 4 large, or 6 small), halved
3 tablespoons (45 mL) tomato puree
3 tablespoons (45 mL) water
¼ cup (60 mL) grated Parmesan or Romano cheese (optional)

Directions:
Melt ¼ cup butter in a large saucepan; then add half the onion and sauté for 1 to 2 minutes. Stir in rice and broth; season with salt and pepper. Reduce heat, and cook until rice is tender, about 20 minutes.

Heat remaining ¼ cup butter in frying pan, and add remaining onion; sauté 1 or 2 minutes. Add sausage and chicken livers; fry 5 minutes over medium heat. Mix tomato puree with water; pour over meat. Cover and simmer over low heat 20 minutes. Place meat in center of warm platter and surround with rice. Sprinkle with cheese, if desired. Yield: 4 to 6 servings.

Italian Spaghetti Sauce

Ingredients:
2 tablespoons (30 mL) butter
1 onion, chopped
1 clove garlic, peeled and cut in half
1 35 oz. (1 L) can of tomatoes
2 tablespoons (30 mL) tomato paste
½ teaspoon (2.5 mL) salt
½ teaspoon (2.5 mL) oregano
½ teaspoon (2.5 mL) basil
¼ teaspoon (1.25 mL) pepper

Directions:
Heat the butter in a saucepan. Add the onion and garlic; cook for 5 to 8 minutes until the onion is pale yellow. Remove the garlic and add the tomatoes and crush them as they cook, using a fork and a spoon. Add the tomato paste and seasonings. Cook uncovered for 20 to 30 minutes. Serve over cooked pasta. Yield: 4 to 6 servings.

Where in the World Are You?

Capital: Sofia
Largest Cities: Sofia, Plovdiv, Varna
Population: 7,537,929 (July 2003 est.)
Land Area: 42,684 sq. mi. (110,550 sq km)
Highest Mountain: Musala (9,596 ft./2,925 m)
Main Languages: Bulgarian
Ethnic Groups: Bulgarian, Turk, Roma
Main Religion: Bulgarian Orthodox, Muslim
Government: Parliamentary democracy
Basic Currency: Lev

The flag consists of three horizontal stripes of white, green, and red.

This country is located on the Balkan Peninsula of southeastern Europe. It is bordered by Romania on the north, Greece and Turkey on the south, and the Black Sea on the east. The two countries on its western border are Serbia and Montenegro and The Former Yugoslav Republic of Macedonia (F.Y.R.O.M.). It measures 170 miles (274 km) from north to south and 306 miles (492 km) from east to west. Mountains cover most of the country and are divided by fertile plains and valleys.

The country's climate varies from region to region because of differences in the terrain. In January, the average temperatures in the country range from 35° F (2° C) near the Black Sea to 0° F (-17° C) in the central part. In July, however, the average temperature is 75° F (24° C) throughout most of the country. The average yearly precipitation is 25 inches (63 centimeters), but the mountain areas usually receive more than 40 inches (100 centimeters) yearly. Snowfall is usually light except in the mountains.

Today the country is developing; however, under Communist rule, its economy was based on government ownership of factories, mines, most farmland, and other resources used for production. Poor management and shortages of fuel and skilled labor slowed economic growth. After the reform government came to power in 1989, it redistributed much of the land in the large government-owned farms to private owners. Manufacturing, mining, and energy production account for about half of the country's net material product and employ about a third of the nation's workers. The top manufacturing industries make chemicals, processed foods, metal products, machinery and textiles. The nation mines coal, copper, kaolin, and lead. Grain is the country's chief farm product. Wheat and corn are the leading grains. Farmers also grow a wide variety of fruits and vegetables.

The people enjoy informal gatherings with friends or relatives. Movies, books, music, and dance styles from Western countries are popular, especially with young people. Sporting events, particularly soccer matches, attract many spectators. Basketball and skiing are also popular. The people in this country enjoy simple stews and other dishes that contain lamb, pork, or beef. Yogurt is a popular part of their diet. Moussaka is a popular dish made with pork or lamb, tomatoes, potatoes, and yogurt. Another popular dish, sarmi, is made with pepper or cabbage stuffed with pork and rice. Perhaps the favorite dessert is baklava, a thin, flaky pastry with a syrup and nut filling.

Where in the world are you?

Political Map of Bulgaria

Directions: Use the map of Bulgaria to answer the questions. Circle the correct answers.

1. The capital city of Bulgaria is _____.
   - a. Nesebur
   - b. Varna
   - c. Sofia
   - d. Pleven

2. All of the following cities except _____ are located on the Black Sea coast.
   - a. Varna
   - b. Nesebur
   - c. Ruse
   - d. Burgas

3. The country of _____ is located to the north of Bulgaria.
   - a. Turkey
   - b. Romania
   - c. Greece
   - d. Serbia and Montenegro

4. The city of _____ is located along the Danube River.
   - a. Ruse
   - b. Pleven
   - c. Varna
   - d. Nesebur

5. The distance between Pleven and Ruse is approximately _____.
   - a. 150 kilometers
   - b. 100 miles
   - c. 50 kilometers
   - d. 100 kilometers

Bulgaria Word Search

Directions: Find the hidden words within the grid of letters.

```
V C A N S V I H V Z I J F Z Z I V P D A
A X G E D R Y T X X P G V M U E L N K S
R R G Z S A H Z Q Q A I E I I O A A I Z
N B N V R K N Y F O S O Y M V L S U G M
A A D S U E C U U X W E R D U S X J P V
J A D W C O C A B I M A I S U C C I U G
A K A F H P J C L E S V N O A J K D F K
F I X P P C Q U O B R I M V O K F U B W
X J N X P U T K J S N I T Y L C F U Z X
B A E T D J A K Q E J V A K M J P C A
A V Y L L T E F P L G P K E U C G O R E
D U L Q J I E N L I C O O A R P P A N U
V V D U D G A A P X A M G D V S Q W I U
Y F L Z N K B O G H J Q Y J O A O E G Z
F G U I L T L T F U I I E L V H L F M L
L Y I A E Z E H V R Q B U K N M R K I G
N K B K F I W I X I V X V X S N E U A A
S X S N M U S H N I M J B E B V V E L B
R A R F H H P E E J K A E P A L A S U M
B D E V E L O P I N G X V S X H P Q V U
```

BAKLAVA	LEV	SKIING
BALKAN PENINSULA	MOUSSAKA	SOCCER
BASKETBALL	MUSALA PEAK	SOFIA
BLACK SEA	PLOVDIV	DEVELOPING
DANUBE RIVER	RHODOPE	VARNA
	SARMI	

Where in the World Are You?

Capital: Moscow

Largest Cities: Moscow, St. Petersburg

Population: 144,526,278 (July 2003 est.)

Land Area: 6,562,121 sq. mi. (16,995,800 sq km)

Highest Mountain: Mount Elbrus (18,481 ft./5633 m)

Main Languages: Russian

Ethnic Groups: Russians, Tatars, Ukrainians

Main Religion: Russian Orthodox

Government: Federation

Basic Currency: Ruble

The flag consists of three horizontal stripes of white, blue, and red.

Here we are in the largest country in the world. Almost twice as big as the second largest country, Canada, it covers much of Asia and Europe. At the widest points, from east to west, it measures 6,000 miles (9,650 kilometers) and from north to south, 2,800 miles (4,500 kilometers). This country extends from the Arctic Ocean south to the Black Sea and from the Baltic Sea east to the Pacific Ocean. The world's deepest lake, Lake Baikal (5,315 ft./1,620 m) at its deepest point is located in Siberia. Lake Ladoga, Europe's largest lake, is located near St. Petersburg and is approximately 6,835 sq. mi. (17,703 sq km). The country's longest river, Lena River, measures 2,734 miles (4,400 m) in length. The capital and largest city is Moscow. If you traveled by train from Moscow in the west to Vladivostok in the east, you would pass through eight time zones and the trip would take seven days. St. Petersburg, the chief seaport, is located on the coast of the Baltic Sea. This city contains the Hermitage Museum, where one of the world's largest art collections is housed.

Czars (emperors) and empresses ruled this country for hundreds of years. They had almost complete control over most people's lives. During their rule, most of the people were poor, unedu-cated peasants. The government was overthrown by revolutionaries in 1917. This country then became communist until 1991. Communist rule ended and the Republic broke apart.

From this country, many great contributions have been made to the arts. Authors, including Tolstoy and Dostoevsky, wrote masterpieces of literature. Musical composers, such as Rimsky-Korsakov and Tchaikovsky, created pieces of lasting beauty. Other contributions have been made in the fields of architecture, ballet, and painting.

Soccer is the most popular sport for spectators and participants. Other popular sports include basketball, gymnastics, hockey, skiing, ice skating and tennis. The people enjoy watching television, playing chess, seeing motion pictures and plays, and visiting museums.

It is not uncommon for there to be food shortages in the cities. This is also true for many manufactured goods. In rural areas, food is plentiful but there is not much variety. Bread, meat, and potatoes are favorite foods in this country. Some popular dishes are borscht (beet soup), piroshki (stuffed dumplings), and beef stroganoff (strips of beef sauteed with mushrooms and onions in sour cream sauce).

Where in the world are you?

Political Map of Russia

Directions: Use the map of Russia to answer the questions. Circle the correct answers.

1. The capital city of Russia is _____.
   a. Volgograd   b. St. Petersburg   c. Moscow   d. Irkutsk

2. The city of _____ is located along the Lena River.
   a. Yakutsk   b. Norilsk   c. Magadan   d. Omsk

3. The distance from Yakutsk to Magadan is approximately _____.
   a. 500 kilometers   b. 250 miles   c. 750 kilometers   d. 750 miles

4. Moscow is located _____ of the Ural Mountains.
   a. north   b. south   c. east   d. west

5. The city of _____ is located along the coast of Barents Sea.
   a. Magadan   b. Vyborg   c. Murmansk   d. Arkhangel'sk

6. The Lena River empties into _____.
   a. Barents Sea   b. Arctic Ocean   c. Bering Sea   d. Pacific Ocean.

Livestock in Russia

Directions: Use the graph to answer the questions. Circle the correct answers.

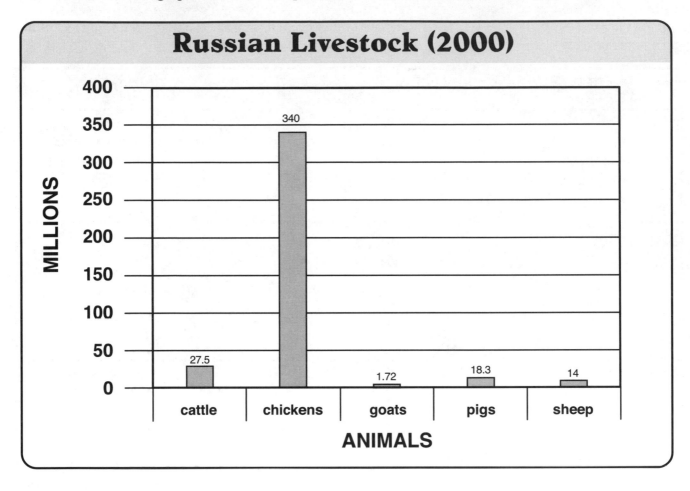

Russian Livestock (2000)

MILLIONS

400
350 — 340
300
250
200
150
100
50 — 27.5
0

| cattle | chickens | goats | pigs | sheep |

27.5 — cattle, 1.72 — goats, 18.3 — pigs, 14 — sheep

ANIMALS

1. Russia produces more _____ than cattle.
   - a. goats
   - b. chickens
   - c. pigs
   - d. sheep.

2. How many more pigs were produced than sheep?
   - a. 17.72 million
   - b. 9.2 million
   - c. 4.3 million
   - d. 32.3 million

3. Russia produces less _____ than sheep.
   - a. goats
   - b. chickens
   - c. pigs
   - d. cattle

4. What is the total number of cattle, goats, and pigs produced in Russia?
   - a. 29.22 million
   - b. 15.72 million
   - c. 47.52 million
   - d. 9.2 million

5. What is the difference between the number of chickens and cattle produced?
   - a. 367.5 million
   - b. 312.5 million
   - c. 615 million
   - d. 165 million

European Quiz!

Directions: Let's play European Quiz! The answers have been given. It is your task to provide the questions. Try to answer as many as possible. Then, use the *Where in the World Are You?* pages to complete the other boxes. When you have completed European Quiz, use the dollar values on the left to determine your winnings!

	Country Capital	Geography	Largest Cities	Famous Foods	Potpourri
$100	The capital city, Paris, has been a world center of art and learning.	country that extends from the Arctic Ocean to the Black Sea and covers much of two continents	the largest city in Russia	A favorite dish of this country is wiener schnitzel.	The highest mountain in this country is Mount Kebnekaise.
$200	Rome, the capital city, was once the center of the Roman Empire.	country that is located between Norway and Finland	the largest city in France	In this country, sometimes a course of antipasto is served before the meal.	Europe's deepest lake, Lake Ladoga, is found in this country.
$300	The capital of this country is Stockholm.	third largest European country in area and shares borders with eight other countries	the largest city in Italy	This country's specialty is bouillabaisse.	The literacy rate in this country is 100%.
$400	Czars once ruled this country whose capital city is Moscow.	Two independent states lie within the country's borders.	the largest city in Sweden	Moussaka is a popular dish in this country.	The Louvre, the Eiffel Tower, and Notre Dame are located in this country.
$500	Many art galleries and concert halls attract tourists to the capital city Vienna.	Located on the Balkan Peninsula, it is bordered by Greece, Turkey, Yugoslavia and Macedonia.	the largest city in Bulgaria	This country is famous for its smorgasboard.	The Danube River borders this country on the north.
$600	The capital city of this country is Sofia.	A landlocked country, it shares borders with Switzerland, Italy, Germany, Slovenia, and the Czech Republic.	the largest city in Austria	Favorite dishes of this country include borscht and piroshki.	The islands of Sicily and Sardinia are part of this country.

Physical Geography of Asia

Location:

The world's largest continent, Asia, is located in the eastern hemisphere. Asia is east of Europe and Africa and northwest of Australia. It is bordered by the Arctic Ocean in the north, the Indian Ocean, the Bay of Bengal and the Arabian Sea in the south, and the Pacific Ocean in the east. The continent covers more than 17,200,000 sq. mi. (44,500,000 sq km). This continent makes up approximately one third of the world's total land area.

Area:

Asia is almost five times larger than the United States. The continent stretches over 5,400 mi. (8,700 km) from north to south and approximately 6,000 mi. (9,700 km) from east to west. The highest point, Mount Everest, the world's tallest mountain, is 29,028 ft. (8,848 m). The world's lowest point is found along the shore of the Dead Sea. It measures 1,310 ft. (399 m) below sea level.

Landforms:

A wide range of natural features can be found in Asia. Among Asia's most famous mountains and mountain ranges are the Himalayas, the world's highest mountains. Mount Everest, the world's highest mountain, is located in this mountain chain. The Hindu Kush, Tien Shan, and Zagros are other important ranges found in Asia.

Other major features of the Asian continent are deserts. The most famous and largest desert in Asia is the Gobi. This desert is the second largest in the world, measuring approximately 500,000 sq. mi. (1,300,000 sq km) and located in northern China and Mongolia. A large portion of southwest Asia is covered by deserts, including the Syrian Desert and the Rub al Khali.

From the mountains of Asia, many long and important rivers flow.

The Yangtze (Chang), the continent's longest river, covers approximately 4,000 mi. (6,400 km). Other major rivers include the Huang, Indus, Ganges, Tigris, and the Euphrates. Many ancient civilizations developed near these rivers.

Numerous plateaus are found in Asia. Most of Turkey is covered by the Plateau of Anatolia. The Deccan Plateau is located in the southern part of India. The Plateau of Tibet is a huge, rocky, and cold one located north of the Himalayas.

The Caspian Sea (143,250 sq. mi./371,000 sq km), the largest lake in the world, and Lake Baikal (5,300 ft./1,600 m), the deepest lake in the world, are both found in Asia. The Dead Sea is a large salt water lake located in southwestern Asia.

Another important feature of the Asian continent is its numerous islands. Many countries in east and southeast Asia are made of groups of islands, such as Japan and the Philippines. Sumatra, Borneo, and Honshu are among the 10 largest islands in the world.

Climate:

The continent of Asia is so large that the climate varies greatly. Southeastern Asia is usually hot year round with much precipitation. In central and southwest Asia, there are deserts with long hot summers, little precipitation, and mild winters. Eastern Asia has cold winters, warm or hot summers, and a medium amount of precipitation. Northern Asia has long, very cold winters.

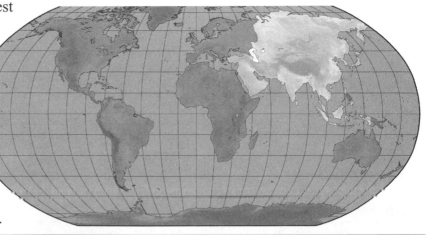

Physical Map of Asia

Directions: Using an atlas, study the physical map of Asia and match the following features with the letters shown on the map.

_____ 1. Rub al Khali

_____ 2. Himalaya Mountains

_____ 3. Ural Mountains

_____ 4. Tien Shan

_____ 5. Zagros Mountains

_____ 6. Syrian Desert

_____ 7. Gobi Desert

_____ 8. Deccan Plateau

_____ 9. Mount Fujiyami

_____ 10. Indian Ocean

_____ 11. Arctic Ocean

_____ 12. Bay of Bengal

_____ 13. Arabian Sea

_____ 14. Pacific Ocean

_____ 15. Caspian Sea

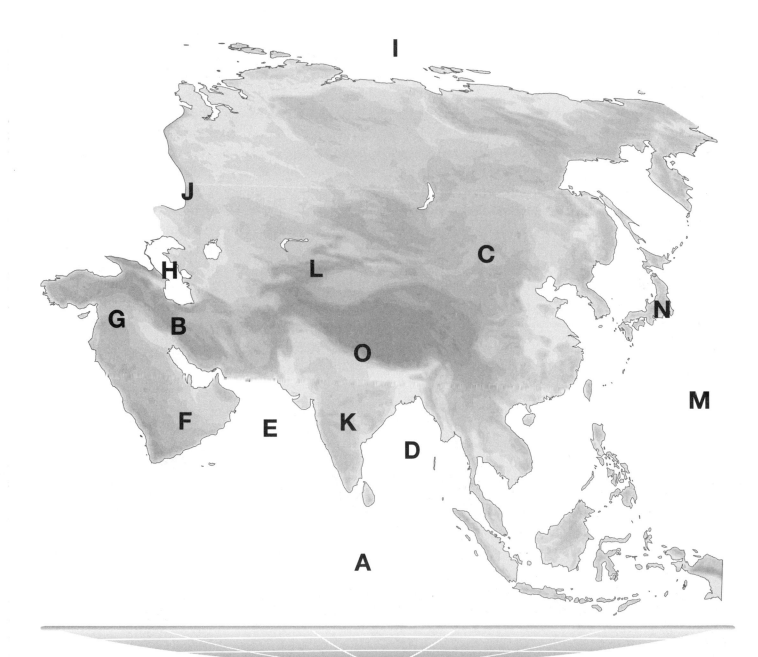

Where in the World Are You?

Capital: Tokyo
Largest Cities: Tokyo, Yokohama, Osaka
Population: 127,214,499 (July 2003 est.)
Land Area: 144,689 sq. mi. (374,744 sq km)
Highest Mountain: Mount Fuji (12,388 ft./3,776 m)
Main Languages: Japanese
Ethnic Groups: Japanese
Main Religions: Shinto, Buddhist
Government: Constitutional monarchy with a parliamentary government
Basic Currency: Yen

This flag features a red circle on a white background.

An island country in the North Pacific Ocean, it lies off the east coast of mainland Asia across from Russia, Korea, and China. Four large islands and thousands of smaller islands make up this country. The four major islands—Hokkaido, Honshu, Kyushu, and Shikoku—form a curve that extends for about 1,200 miles (1,900 kilometers). About 126 million people are crowded on these islands, making this country one of the most densely populated in the world. Mountains and hills cover most of the country, taking up a large area of land. The great majority of the people live on a small portion of the land. The coastal plains have much of the country's best farmland and most of the country's major cities. Most of the people live in urban areas. Toyko, the capital, is the largest city.

Climates vary from island to island. Honshu generally has warm, humid summers with balmy, sunny autumns and springs. Hokkaido has cool summers and cold winters. Kyushu and Shikoku have long, hot summers and mild winters. Seasonal winds called monsoons also affect the climate. Summer monsoons carry warm moist air from the Pacific Ocean and cause hot, humid weather in the central and southern parts of the country. Earthquakes are quite common here with an average of 1,500 per year; however, most of the earthquakes are minor.

The size of this country's economy ranks second to that of the United States in terms of gross domestic product (GDP). It is one of the world's leading countries in value of its exports and imports. On average, the families enjoy one of the highest income levels in the world. Key elements of their economy are manufacturing and trade. Some well-known companies include Nissan Motor Company, Sony Corporation, Toshiba Corporation, and Toyota Motor Corporation. The country has few natural resources so it must buy such necessities as aluminum, coal, lead, and petroleum. Agriculture represents a small portion of the economy. Farmers grow some crops on terraced fields—level strips of land cut out of hillsides. Farmers are able to produce all of the eggs, potatoes, rice and fresh vegetables eaten.

The people are quite enthusiastic about sports. School children are encouraged to participate in a variety of sports, such as bowling, golf, baseball, gymnastics, and tennis. Another popular sport, kendo, is a form of fencing using bamboo or wooden sticks for swords. Traditional martial arts, aikido, judo, and karate, involve fighting without weapons and are practiced by many people.

Where in the world are you?

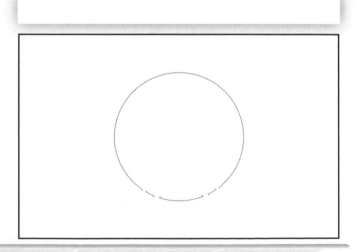

Political Map of Japan

Directions: Use the map of Japan to answer the questions. Circle the correct answers.

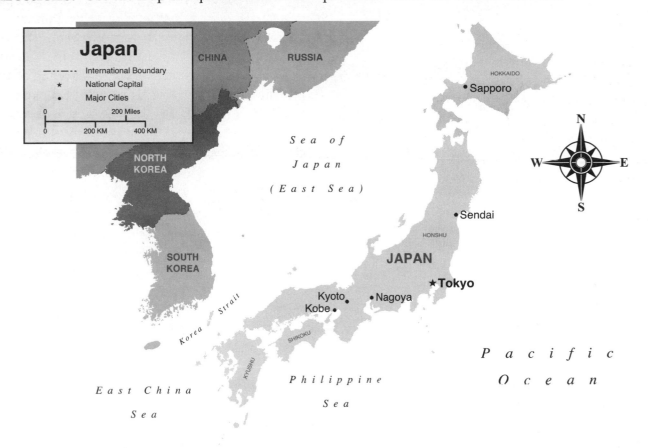

1. The body of water located south of the Japanese islands is _____.
    a. Sea of Japan   b. Korea Strait   c. Philippine Sea   d. East China Sea

2. The distance between Kobe and Tokyo is approximately _____.
    a. 400 kilometers   b. 100 kilometers   c. 600 kilometers   d. 200 kilometers

3. The island of Hokkaido is located _____ of the island of Honshu.
    a. north   b. south   c. east   d. west

4. The capital city of Japan is _____.
    a. Akita   b. Sapporo   c. Sendai   d. Tokyo

5. The island of Kyushu is located _____ of South Korea.
    a. northeast   b. northwest   c. southeast   d. southwest

6. The distance between Nagoya and Kyoto is approximately _____.
    a. 200 miles   b. 100 kilometers   c. 400 kilometers   d. 200 kilometers

How to Make Japanese Streamers

Origami is the Japanese art of paper folding. There are two kinds of origami—creative and traditional. Both kinds can be found in many parts of the world. While the traditional is more appealing to children, the creative is more popular with adults. The following activity, making Japanese streamers, is a form of origami.

Materials:
18 squares of origami paper, 4½″ square (11.5 cm)
A dowel or a stick approximately 24 inches (60 cm) long
Three pieces of thin string or thread approximately 18 inches (45.5 cm)
Sewing needle
45 beads

Directions:
1. Fold one paper square (colored side in) in half to make a rectangle (crease folds well).
2. Fold the rectangle in half again in order to form a small square.
3. Unfold the paper.
4. Fold in half diagonally to create a triangle. Crease the folds well.
5. Unfold and fold diagonally in half the other way.
6. Open the paper with the colored side up. If done correctly, the paper will be raised from the surface.
7. Take two adjacent corners and put them together. Repeat with the opposite corners. Now you should have back to back triangles when the paper is slightly opened.
8. Repeat the above steps with the other seventeen pieces of paper.
9. Group the triangles into three sets. Using the needle and thread, string six triangles on each piece of string. Put three beads in between each triangle to separate them. Line up the flaps of the triangles so that they fit into the triangle below. Tie the strings to the dowel or stick.

1. 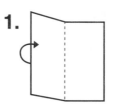 **2.**   **3.**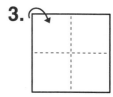

4. 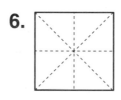 **5.**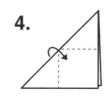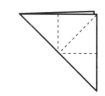

6. 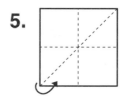 **7-8.**

9.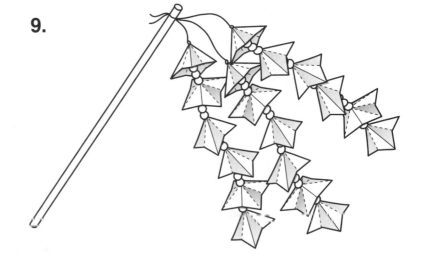

Where in the World Are You?

Capital: Beijing

Largest Cities: Shanghai, Beijing, Tianjin, Shenyang, Wuhan, Guangzhou

Population: 1,286,975,468 (July 2003 est.)

Land Area: 3,600,950 sq. mi. (9,326,410 sq km)

Highest Mountain: Mount Everest (29,035 ft./ 8,850 m)

Main Language: Standard Chinese (Mandarin)

Ethnic Group: Han Chinese

Main Religions: Daoist (Taoist), Buddhist (officially atheist)

Government: Communist state

Basic Currency: Yuan

This flag has five yellow stars on a bright red background. The large star stands for the Community Party. The smaller stars represent the four classes of society.

Located on the continent of Asia, it is the world's third largest country in size and the most populated country on Earth. The country covers more than one-fifth of Asia. The country's vast land area includes some of the world's driest deserts and highest mountains, as well as some of the richest farmland. Mount Everest, the highest mountain in the world, is part of the Himalayan mountain range.

Most people live in densely populated areas in the eastern third of the country. This part of the country has most major cities and nearly all of the land suitable for farming. About 74% of the people live in rural villages, and about 60% of all workers are farmers. The main products are rice, wheat, cotton, tobacco, and silk. This country has some of the largest cities in the world—Shanghai and Beijing, the nation's capital.

The world's oldest living civilization, this country's written history goes back about 3,500 years. The people take great pride in their nation, its long history, and its influence on other countries. They were the first to develop the compass, paper, porcelain, and silk cloth.

Because the country is so large and its landscape so diverse, it has a broad range of contrasting climates. The most dramatic conditions occur in the Taklimakan and Gobi deserts. Daytime temperatures in these deserts may exceed 100° F (38° C) in summer, but nighttime lows may fall to -30° F (-34° C) in winter. Both Tibet and northern Manchuria have long, bitterly cold winters. In contrast, southeastern coastal areas have a tropical climate. Seasonal winds, or monsoons, also affect the climate.

The people of this country have always prized education and respected scholars. Today, the Communists regard education as a key to reaching their political, social, and economic goals. The literacy rate for age 15 and older is approximately 70%. Children must attend school for nine years, beginning at age six or seven.

Grains are the main foods in this country. Rice is the favorite grain among people in the south. In the north, people prefer wheat, which they make into bread and noodles. Vegetables, especially cabbages and tofu (soybean curd), rank second in the diet. Pork and poultry are favorite meats. A typical main meal includes vegetables with bits of meat or seafood, soup, and rice or noodles. Chopsticks and soup spoons serve as the only utensils at their meals. Tea is the traditional favorite beverage.

Where in the world are you?

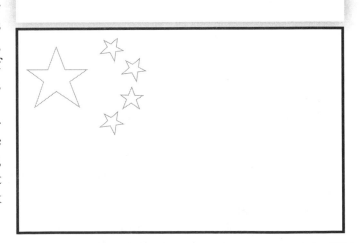

Political Map of China

Directions: Use the map of China to answer the questions. Circle the correct answers.

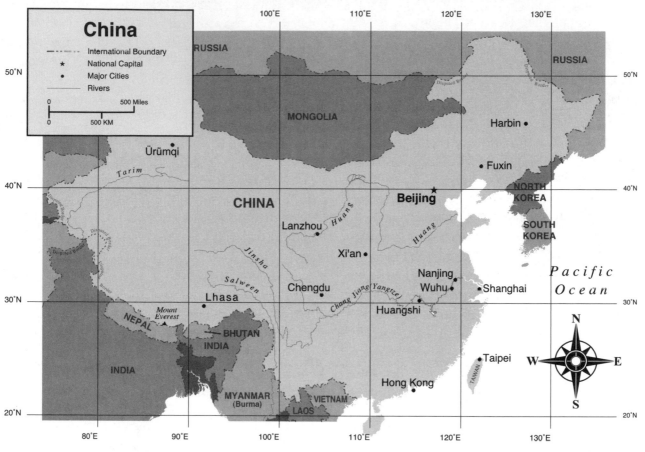

1. The capital city of Beijing is located along the _____° line of latitude.
   a. 20   b. 40   c. 130   d. 145

2. The Chang Jiang River (Yangtze) runs through the city of _____.
   a. Chengdu   b. Lhasa   c. Wuhu   d. Harbin

3. The distance from Beijing to Fuxin is approximately _____.
   a. 500 kilometers   b. 800 kilometers   c. 800 miles   d. 100 miles

4. The city of _____ is located along the East China Sea coast.
   a. Urumqi   b. Nanjing   c. Chengdu   d. Shanghai

5. Mount Everest is located _____ of Beijing.
   a. northeast   b. northwest   c. southeast   d. southwest

6. The country of _____ is north of China.
   a. Vietnam   b. India   c. Mongolia   d. Myanmar (Burma)

Population Growth in China

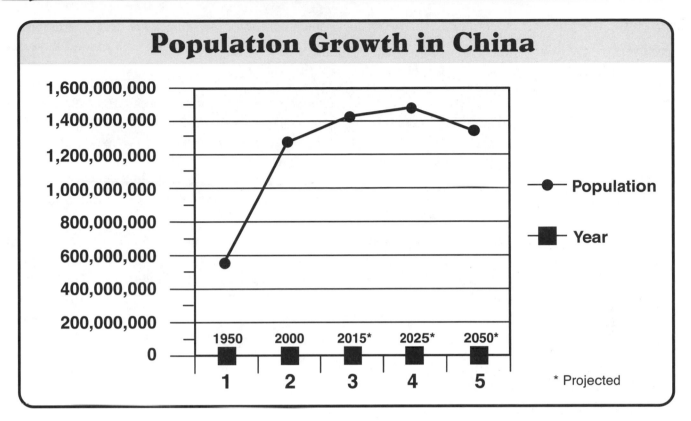

Population Growth in China

Chart showing population values on y-axis (0 to 1,600,000,000) and years on x-axis: 1950, 2000, 2015, 2025*, 2050* (positions 1-5)*

Legend: ● Population, ■ Year

* Projected

Directions: Study the graph above and answer the following questions. Circle the correct answers.

1. China's population in 1950 was _____ 600,000,000.
   - a. more than
   - b. twice
   - c. less than
   - d. equal to

2. This population graph projects that China's population will decrease after the year _____.
   - a. 2000
   - b. 2005
   - c. 2025
   - d. 2015

3. The population in China in 2050 is predicted to _____ from 2025.
   - a. double
   - b. triple
   - c. decrease
   - d. increase by 1,000,000

4. The period that the population reached 1,000,000,000 was between _____ and _____.
   - a. 1950, 2000
   - b. 2000, 2015
   - c. 2025, 2050
   - d. 2015, 2025

5. The projected population in China in the year 2025 will be almost _____.
   - a. 600,000,000
   - b. 1,200,000,000
   - c. 1,500,000,000
   - d. 200,000,000

6. The population in the year 1950 was approximately _____.
   - a. 700,000,000
   - b. 550,000,000
   - c. 1,350,000,000
   - d. 350,000,000

Where in the World Are You?

Capital: New Delhi

Largest Cities: Mumbai (Bombay), Delhi, Kolkata (Calcutta)

Population: 1,049,700,118 (July 2003 est.)

Land Area: 1,147,960 sq. mi. (2,973,190 sq km)

Highest Mountain: Kanchenjunga (28,208 ft./ 8,598 m)

Main Languages: Hindi, English

Ethnic Groups: Indo-Aryans, Dravidians

Main Religions: Hindu, Muslim, Christian, Sikh

Government: Federal republic

Basic Currency: Rupee

The flag has three horizontal stripes of orange-yellow, white, and green. A wheel, an ancient symbol call the Dharma Chakra, is centered on the white stripe.

Located in southern Asia, this country ranks second in total population. This country is bordered on the west by the Arabian Sea and Pakistan, on the north by China, Nepal, and Bhutan, and on the east by Myanmar (formerly known as Burma), Bangladesh, and the Bay of Bengal. From north to south, it stretches 2,000 miles (3,200 km) and 1,700 miles (2,746 km) from east to west. From the snow-capped Himalayas to the Thar Desert, to the Deccan Plateau, and to the Northern Plains, this country is a land of great contrasts and variety. One of the world's longest rivers, the Ganges, is considered sacred by the Hindus.

This country is so large and varied that there is no one way of life practiced by all of the people. Throughout the country clothing and food vary. A number of religious beliefs and practices are followed by the people. Cows are sacred in the Hindu religion. In fact, this country has more cattle than any other country in the world. However, there are some common features among most people of the country. Family ties are important in most areas. Extended families of three generations live together in some households. Marriages are usually arranged by parents. Most people live in villages and have few possessions.

The main source of income for the majority of the people is agriculture. About half of the country's land is covered with farmland. Approximately three-fourths of this farmland is used to grow pulses (seeds, lentils, and beans) and grains. This country is a leading producer of cotton, jute, sugarcane, millet, and tea. It is one of the world's top producers of iron and steel.

Cricket, field hockey, and soccer are popular sports. Chess and playing cards are also enjoyed by the people of this country. Another common recreational activity is kite flying. The film industry in this country is one of the world's largest. One popular form of entertainment is attending the movies. Many cities have over one hundred movie theaters.

The grandson of one of the greatest Mughal emperors, Shah Jahan, was responsible for the building of one of the most famous and beautiful buildings in the world, the Taj Mahal, built between 1632 and 1653. It was built as a tomb for Shah Jahan's wife and now houses his body.

Where in the world are you?

Political Map of India

Directions: Use the map of India to answer the questions. Circle the correct answers.

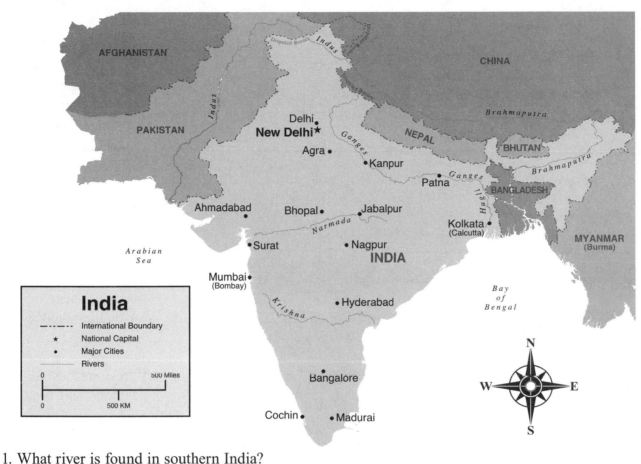

1. What river is found in southern India?
   - a. Indus
   - b. Brahmaputra
   - c. Ganges
   - d. Krishna

2. All of the following cities are located on the Arabian Sea coast except _____.
   - a. Mumbai
   - b. Cochin
   - c. Surat
   - d. Agra

3. The distance between Surat and Bhopal is approximately _____.
   - a. 500 kilometers
   - b. 200 kilometers
   - c. 200 miles
   - d. 500 miles

4. The capital city of India is _____.
   - a. Hyderabad
   - b. New Delhi
   - c. Agra
   - d. Nagpur

5. The city of _____ is located along the Ganges River.
   - a. Madurai
   - b. Jabalpur
   - c. Kanpur
   - d. Bangalore

6. The city of Ahmadabad is almost directly _____ of Bhopal.
   - a. north
   - b. south
   - c. east
   - d. west

Double Puzzle on India

Directions: Unscramble the following words by placing the letters in the blanks provided. Use the numbered letters to solve the second puzzle.

WNE DLIHE ___ _____
4

BAOYBM _____
13

AHAILASYM _____
27   1

TARH REDTES ____ _____
9 28 19

EDCANC PULTAAE _____ _____
21   11

EGGNSA _____
7

HUNISD _____
18

LUSEPS _____
20

CKTRECI _____
12 8   29

DFILE KCHOEY _____ _____
23   5   30

IKTE LIYFNG ____ _____
15   6

LMFI YDUNTIRS ____ _____
14   16

AHSH JNHAA ____ _____
2   17 22

TJA AMAHL ___ _____
25 10

DIDASVIANR _____
26 24   3

_ _ _ _ _ _   _ _ _ _ _ _   _ _ _ _ _ _ _ _ _ _ _   _ _ _
1 2 3 4   5 6   7 8 9 10 11   12 13 14 15 16 17 18 19 20   21 22 23

_ _ _ _ _ _ _
24 25 26 27 28 29 30

Where in the World Are You?

Capital: Riyadh

Largest Cities: Riyadh, Jidda, Mecca

Population: 24,293,844 (July 2003 est.)

Land Area: 756,985 sq. mi. (1,960,582 sq km)

Highest Mountain: Jabal Sawda (10,279 ft./3,133 m)

Main Language: Arabic

Ethnic Group: Arab

Main Religion: Muslim

Government: Monarchy

Basic Currency: Riyal

The flag is green with an Arabic message in white script above a white sword. The Arabic words state: "There is no God but Allah and Mohammed is his Prophet."

The largest country on the Arabian Peninsula, it is the world's twelfth largest country. Much of the country consists of vast deserts where few people live and little or nothing grows; however, beneath the sand and rock and the offshore waters lie some of the largest petroleum deposits in the world. The country measures 1,145 miles (1,843 km) from north to south and 1,290 miles (2,076 km) from east to west. The country is bordered by Jordan, Iraq, and Kuwait to the north; the Persian Gulf and the United Arab Emirates to the east; Oman and Yemen to the south; and the Red Sea to the west. Riyadh is the capital and the largest city. The world's largest sand desert, Rub al Khali, covers 250,000 sq. mi. (647,500 sq km) in the southern part.

Most of the country is hot year-round. The coastal regions are hot and humid during the long summers, when the average daytime temperature is over 90° F (32° C). In the central plateau and the desert regions, temperatures in the summer may reach 120° F (49° C). These areas, however, have drier air and cool nights. Asir is the only part of the country that receives significant rainfall with an average rainfall of 12-20 inches (30-51 cm) per year. The remainder of the country receives less than 4 inches (10 cm) annually. A northwesterly wind, called the shamal, causes frequent sandstorms in the eastern part of the country.

This nation has experienced a period of rapid development since the price of oil rose sharply in the mid-1970's. The richest oil fields are in the Eastern Province and in the Persian Gulf. Since this country has no permanent rivers or bodies of fresh water, obtaining adequate fresh water has been a constant challenge. The main source of water for agriculture is a huge reservoir that runs underground from the eastern highlands of Turkey. Only about 1% of the land is used to grow crops. Farmers grow a number of crops, including barley, citrus fruits, dates, millet, sorghum, and tomatoes. The farmers cannot produce all of the food the country needs. As a result, the country imports a large percentage of its food.

A majority of the people 15 years of age or older can read and write. The government provides free schooling for citizens at all levels of education. School attendance is not required by law. The first public schools were established in 1951, for boys only. Public education for girls began in 1960. Today, more than 80% of children of primary school age attend school, and boys and girls are enrolled in almost equal numbers. In public schools, boys and girls study a similar curriculum.

Where in the world are you?

Political Map of Saudi Arabia

Directions: Use the map of Saudi Arabia to answer the questions. Circle the correct answers.

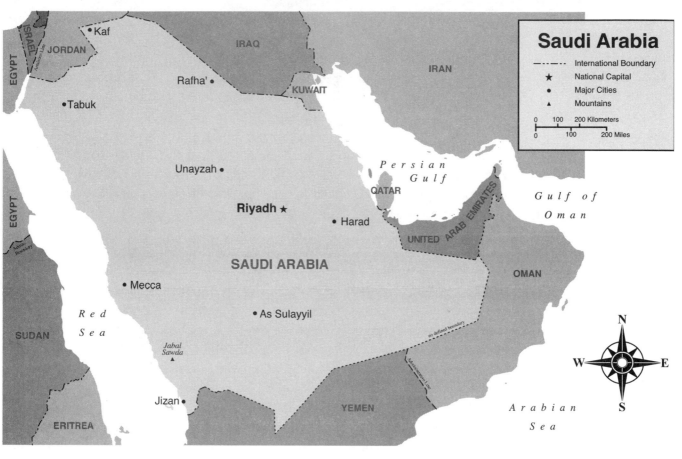

1. The body of water located west of Saudi Arabia is _____.
   a. Persian Gulf   b. Arabian Sea   c. Red Sea   d. Jordan River

2. The distance between Riyadh and Unayzah is approximately _____.
   a. 200 miles   b. 100 miles   c. 300 miles   d. 400 miles

3. The country of _____ is due south of Saudi Arabia.
   a. Iran   b. Yemen   c. Iraq   d. Jordan

4. The mountain Jabal Sawda is located in the _____ part of Saudi Arabia.
   a. northeastern   b. southeastern   c. northwestern   d. southwestern

5. The distance between Tabuk and Rafha' is approximately _____.
   a. 400 miles   b. 200 kilometers   c. 100 kilometers   d. 200 miles

Using the Arabic Alphabet

Directions: Study the Arabic alphabet given below. Then, practice writing the alphabet in the space provided.

Alif	ا	Za	ز	Pha	ف
Ba	ب	Sín	س	Khaf	ق
Ta	ت	Shin	ش	Khif	ك
Sa	ث	Saad	ص	Lam	ل
Jem	ج	Daad	ض	Mim	م
Ha	ح	Tau	ط	Noon	ن
Kha	خ	Zau	ظ	Ha	ه
Dal	د	Eyn	ع	Waw	و
Zal	ذ	Ghyn	غ	Ya	ي
Ra	ر				

Where in the World Are You?

Capital: Bangkok

Largest Cities: Bangkok, Chiang Mai

Population: 64,265,276 (July 2003 est.)

Land Area: 197,596 sq. mi. (511,770 sq km)

Highest Mountain: Doi Inthanon (8,451 ft./2,576 m)

Main Languages: Thai, English

Ethnic Groups: Thai, Chinese

Main Religions: Buddhist, Muslim

Government: Constitutional monarchy

Basic Currency: Baht

The flag has five horizontal stripes of red, white, blue, white, and red. Red, white, and blue represent the nation, purity, and the monarchy, accordingly.

A tropical country in Southeast Asia, it is the only nation that has never been ruled by a Western power. It measures 1,100 miles (1,770 km) from north to south and 480 miles (772 km) from east to west, and has 1,635 miles (2,631 km) of coastline.

The country has four main land regions: In the northern mountains, many streams flow south from the mountains. Doi Inthanon, the country's highest peak, is in this region. Rice is grown in the valleys, and the region has rich mineral deposits. The Khorat Plateau in the eastern part covers 30% of the country's area and is most heavily populated. The central plain is located between the foothills of the northern mountains and the gulf. The Mekong River forms the region's northern and eastern boundaries. Farmers grow more rice here than in any other part of the country. The southern peninsula shares it northwestern border with Myanmar and extends south to Malaysia. This region consists mainly of jungles and mountains. Fishing, rubber production, and tin mining contribute much to the economy.

The country has a tropical climate. Most of the country has three seasons—a hot, dry season from March to May; a hot, wet period from June to October; and a cool, dry season from November to mid-March caused by the northeast monsoons (winds). The southern isthmus remains hot and humid throughout the year. Bangkok has an average temperature of 77° F (25° C) in December and 86° F (30° C) in April. It has an average rainfall of 55 inches (140 cm).

Each village has a wat (Buddhist temple-monastery), which serves as the religious and social center of each community. Village life traditionally has been organized around religious and agricultural rituals and festivals. Now radio and television have a strong influence. Since the 1960's, large numbers of young adults have moved from rural areas to cities in search of jobs and educational opportunities. As a result, a large educated middle class has emerged in Bangkok and other cities. The cities have had to cope with serious problems caused by rapid population growth—crowded living conditions, traffic jams, and pollution.

The people eat rice with almost every meal. Favorite foods to accompany the rice include hot, spicy stews called curries; salads of meat, fish, and vegetables; stir-fried dishes, and broiled or fried fish with sauces. Today, their flavorful, spicy foods have become popular in many parts of the world.

Where in the world are you?

Political Map of Thailand

Directions: Use the map of Thailand to answer the questions. Circle the correct answers.

1. The capital city of Thailand is _____.
   - a. Sattahip
   - b. Khon Kaen
   - c. Nong Khai
   - d. Bangkok

2. The city of _____ is located on the Gulf of Thailand coast.
   - a. Chiang Mai
   - b. Sattahip
   - c. Khon Kaen
   - d. Ubon Ratchathani

3. The _____ lies to the west of Bangkok, Thailand.
   - a. Gulf of Thailand
   - b. Andaman Sea
   - c. South China Sea
   - d. Strait of Malacca

4. Khon Kaen is almost directly _____ of Nong Khai.
   - a. north
   - b. east
   - c. south
   - d. west

5. The Khorat Plateau is located in the _____ part of Thailand.
   - a. northern
   - b. eastern
   - c. southern
   - d. western

6. What country is located southwest of the Strait of Malacca?
   - a. Malaysia
   - b. Cambodia
   - c. Vietnam
   - d. Indonesia

7. The city of _____ is located in northwest Thailand.
   - a. Chiang Mai
   - b. Chumphon
   - c. Bangkok
   - d. Songkhla

A Little Taste of Thailand

Thai Basil Chicken

Ingredients:
1   lb. (454 g) skinned, boned chicken breasts
4   cloves garlic, minced
4   green onions, chopped
2   tablespoons (30 mL) peanut or olive oil
4   tiny green or red chili peppers, stemmed and finely chopped
¾ cup (180 mL) finely chopped fresh basil leaves
2   tablespoons (30 mL) fish sauce

Directions:
Place chicken breasts in the freezer until firm, but not frozen solid. Cut chicken into tiny slivers. Preheat wok; add olive oil, and stir-fry garlic and green onions until tender but not brown, approximately 1-2 minutes. Add chicken and stir-fry until it is cooked. Stir in the basil and fish sauce, mixing quite thoroughly. If desired, serve over rice.

Cucumber Salad

Ingredients:
1   large cucumber, seeds removed
2   cloves garlic, minced
1   small green chili, chopped
2   teaspoons (10 mL) tamarind juice
1   tablespoon (15 mL) Thai fish sauce
1   teaspoon (5 mL) sugar
6   cherry tomatoes, quartered

Directions:
Peel the cucumber and cut into shreds the size of matchsticks; add the tomatoes. Mix together remaining ingredients and pour over salad. Toss to combine. Serve as a side dish to the chicken or vegetable recipe.

Stir Fried Vegetables

Ingredients:
1   cup (240 mL) baby corn
¾ cup (180 mL) button mushrooms
1   cup (240 mL) snow peas, sliced
1   small red chili pepper, cut into thin strips
½ bunch spring onions, cut into 2¼ (5.7 cm) inch pieces
2   cloves garlic, crushed
2   tablespoons (30 mL) oyster sauce
2   tablespoons (30 mL) Thai fish sauce
1   teaspoon (5 mL) sugar
½ teaspoon (2.5 mL) freshly ground black pepper
2   tablespoons (30 mL) vegetable oil

Directions:
Heat the wok. Add oil, and stir-fry snow peas, red pepper, and spring onions until cooked as desired. Next, add baby corn and mushrooms. Stir-fry until thoroughly heated. Add remaining ingredients and toss to combine. You may wish to serve an accompanying dish to the vegetables or just serve over rice.

Asian Agricultural Products

Directions: Read the following graphs and fill in the blanks with the correct answer or answers.

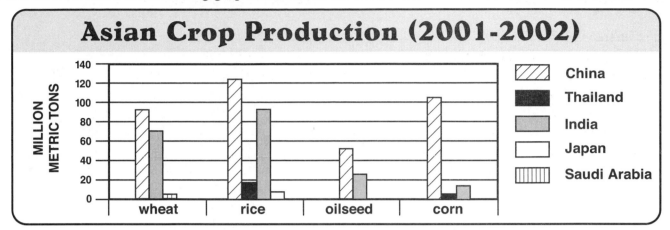

____ 1. Japan and Thailand do not report measurable or significant production of _____ or _____.

     a. rice   b. corn   c. wheat   d. oilseed

____ 2. India produces approximately _____ million metric tons of wheat.

     a. 70   b. 60   c. 90   d. 24

____ 3. Saudi Arabia produces less wheat than _____ and _____.

     a. China   b. Thailand   c. India   d. Japan

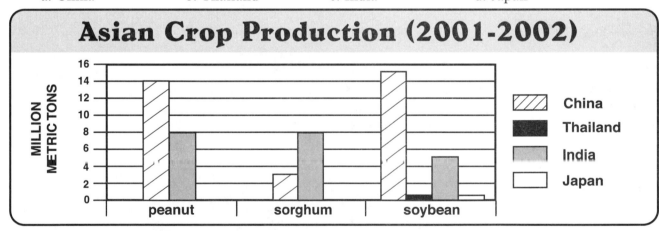

____ 4. Japan and Thailand produce the same amount of _____.

     a. peanuts   b. sorghum   c. soybeans

____ 5. India produces approximately _____ million metric tons of peanuts.

     a. 5   b. 14   c. 8   d. 3

____ 6. China produces approximately 15 million metric tons of _____.

     a. peanuts   b. soybeans   c. sorghum

Physical Geography of Africa

Location:

Almost completely surrounded by water, Africa is located in the eastern hemisphere. About two-thirds of the continent is in the northern hemisphere and one-third is in the southern hemisphere. The equator divides Africa almost in half. The northern coast is bordered by the Mediterranean Sea. The western coast borders the Atlantic Ocean, and the eastern coast is bordered by the Indian Ocean, the Arabian Sea, and the Red Sea. A small peninsula joins Africa to southwest Asia.

Area:

The continent of Africa is slightly more than three times the size of the United States. It is the second largest continent. Africa is about 11,700,000 sq. mi. (30,300,000 sq km) in area. It is about 5,000 miles (8,000 km) from north to south and 4,700 miles (7,600 km) from east to west. The lowest point on the continent is Lake Assal (509 ft./155 m) below sea level. The highest point is Mount Kilimanjaro (19,340 ft./5,895 m). Several islands are included as part of the African continent. The largest island, Madagascar, is located off the southeastern coast.

Landforms:

Most of Africa is a large plateau. On this plateau there are three main landforms—deserts, grasslands, and tropical rain forests. The Sahara, the world's largest desert, is located in northern Africa. This vast desert is spread over 3,500,000 sq. mi. (9,065,000 sq km) and covers one-fourth of the continent. The Namib Desert and the Kalahari Desert are located in southern Africa in the countries of Namibia and Botswana. Approximately two-fifths of Africa is covered by savannahs or grasslands. Most of the grasslands are found between the tropical rain forests and the deserts. Tropical rain forests make up approximately one-fifth

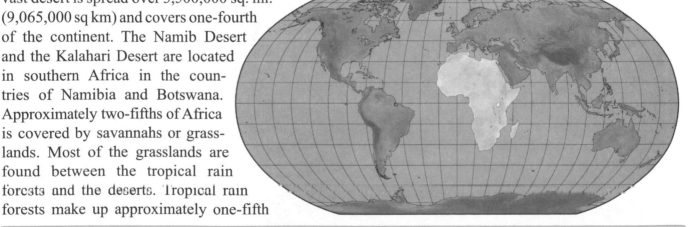

of the continent. Central Africa contains the largest area of rain forests. The island of Madagascar also contains rain forests.

Two important river basins are located in Africa. The Nile River in the northeast corner is the world's longest river. The other river basin includes the Congo River and its tributaries found in central Africa. Lake Tanganyika, the longest fresh-water lake in the world, is found in eastern Africa. The world's third largest lake, Lake Victoria, is also in eastern Africa.

In the eastern part of the continent, there are many steep-sided valleys which were formed by cracks in the earth's surface. They are a part of the Great Rift Valley, one of Africa's most interesting physical features. The Great Rift Valley, which was formed millions of years ago, runs from north to south for hundreds of miles.

Climate:

With a variety of climate conditions, Africa is generally warm or hot. Most of Africa is located in a tropical zone. There are few mountain ranges acting as barriers. Numerous ocean currents keep the climate uniform. Rainfall varies depending on the location. Central Africa receives the heaviest rainfall whereas the northern and southern regions have limited precipitation.

Physical Map of Africa

Directions: Study the physical map of Africa and match the following features with the letters shown on the map.

____ 1. Mount Kilimanjaro

____ 2. Lake Victoria

____ 3. Sahara Desert

____ 4. Nile River

____ 5. Lake Tanganyika

____ 6. Mediterranean Sea

____ 7. Madagascar

____ 8. Namib Desert

____ 9. Congo River

____ 10. Kalahari Desert

____ 11. Atlantic Ocean

____ 12. Atlas Mountains

____ 13. Indian Ocean

____ 14. Red Sea

____ 15. Gulf of Guinea

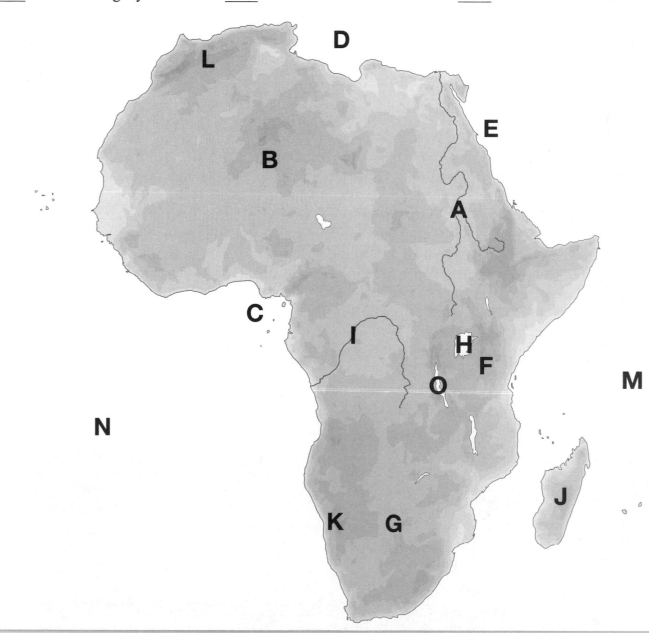

Capital: Rabat
Largest Cities: Casablanca, Marrakech
Population: 31,689,265 (July 2003 Est.)
Land Area: 172,317 sq. mi. (446,300 sq km)
Highest Mountain: Jbel Toubkal (13,665 ft./4,165 m)
Main Languages: Arabic, Berber, French
Ethnic Group: Arab-Berber
Main Religion: Muslim, Christian, Jewish
Government: Constitutional monarchy
Basic Currency: Dirham

The flag consists of a red field with a green five-pointed star in the center.

Located in northwestern Africa, it has snow-capped mountains, beaches, and deserts. It is possible to stand on the shore in the city of Tangier and see Europe, which is only 8½ miles (13.6 km) away. This country is bordered on the west by the Atlantic Ocean, on the north by the Mediterranean Sea, on the east by Algeria, and to the south and west by Mauritania. The country claims the area to the south, which the rest of the world calls the Western Sahara. There are four mountain ranges including the Rif Mountains, the northernmost range; the Middle Atlas Mountains, which nearly overlap the High Atlas; the High Atlas Mountains, the tallest in the country; and the Anti-Atlas Mountains which touch the High Atlas at one end. Between the mountain ranges there are valleys and lowlands. To the east and south of the mountains is the Sahara Desert.

When the country has enough rainfall, it can produce about two-thirds of the food it needs to feed its people. The average amount of rainfall in the country varies from 37.5 in (95 cm) in the north to less than 4 in. (10 cm) in the Sahara region. Barley, citrus fruits, corn, and potatoes are some of the main crops. This is made possible by using modern irrigation techniques and greenhouses. The mining industry is the main source of income for the country. The main mineral is phosphate. The country has about two-thirds of the world's supply. Fishing, especially for sardines, is important. The port city of Agadir is known as the largest sardine-fishing port in the world.

Soccer is the main sport enjoyed by the people. This country has one of the best teams in Africa. Tennis is also an important sport. The citizens proudly participate in the Olympics and won their first medal in the 1984 Olympic Games. Once a year the people enjoy being a part of the Paris-Dakar road rally. Participants begin in Paris, France, travel south through Europe, take a ferry across the Mediterranean, and continue through the country and on to the country of Senegal.

Mint tea is a part of every meal. Usually it is served from a silver teapot. Part of the pleasure of drinking the tea is the art of pouring it. The tea is always poured from high above the glasses, often as far as 2 ft. (61 cm). Many spices are used in cooking. The traditional dish most often served is tajine. It is named for the dish in which it is cooked. It may be made with lamb, chicken or other meat and usually includes prunes, almonds, onions and cinnamon.

Where in the world are you?

Political Map of Morocco

Directions: Use the map of Morocco to answer the questions. Circle the correct answers.

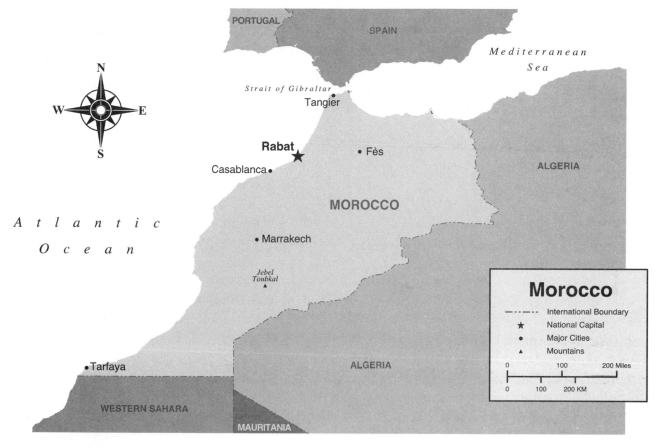

1. The capital of Morocco is _____.
   a. Tangier   b. Rabat   c. Casablanca   d. Marrakech

2. The city that is the farthest north is _____.
   a Marrakech   b. Rabat   c. Tarfaya   d. Tangier

3. The city of _____ is not located along the Atlantic Coast.
   a. Tangier   b. Marrakech   c. Casablanca   d. Rabat

4. The highest point in Morocco, Jebel Toubkal, is located _____ of Marrakech.
   a. north   b. south   c. east   d. west

5. The city of Fès is located approximately _____ east of Rabat.
   a. 100 kilometers   b. 100 miles   c. 200 kilometers   d. 200 miles

6. From Casablanca to Rabat is about _____.
   a. 200 kilometers   b. 200 miles   c. 100 kilometers   d. 150 miles

Matching Moroccan Facts

Directions: Match the following facts about Morocco with the correct terms.

_____ 1. A drink that is part of every meal

_____ 2. One of Morocco's largest cities

_____ 3. From this city you can see Europe

_____ 4. The major religion of Morocco

_____ 5. Morocco's basic currency

_____ 6. The highest mountain in Morocco

_____ 7. Borders Morocco on the north

_____ 8. Morocco's capital city

_____ 9. The main mineral of Morocco

_____ 10. Road rally that passes through Morocco

_____ 11. Desert found in Morocco

_____ 12. Mountains in northern Morocco

_____ 13. Dish made with meat, fruit, and spices.

_____ 14. Country bordering Morocco to the east

_____ 15. Crop grown in Morocco

_____ 16. Type of government in Morocco

_____ 17. Main languages in Morocco

_____ 18. Agadir is known as the largest _____ fishing port in the world.

A. Casablanca

B. Islam

C. Jebel Toubkal

D. Algeria

E. Constitutional monarchy

F. tajine

G. Rabat

H. barley

I. Arabic, Berber

J. sardine

K. phosphate

L. Sahara

M. Tangier

N. mint tea

O. Dirham

P. Rif

Q. Paris-Dakar

R. Mediterranean Sea

Where in the World Are You?

Capital: Cairo

Largest Cities: Cairo, Alexandria, Al Jizah (Giza)

Population: 74,718,797 (July 2003 Est.)

Land Area: 384,345 sq. mi. (995,450 sq km)

Highest Mountain: Jabal Katrinah (Mount Catherine) (8,625 ft./2,629 m)

Main Language: Arabic

Ethnic Group: Egyptian, Bedouin, Berber

Main Religion: Sunni Muslim

Government: Republic

Basic Currency: Pound

The flag has three vertical stripes of red, white, and black with a golden eagle centered in the white stripe.

The Nile River flows through the eastern part of this country from south to north to the Mediterranean Sea. The Red Sea borders it on the east, the Mediterranean Sea to the north, Libya to the west, and Sudan to the south. This country controls the Sinai Peninsula, the only land bridge between Africa and the rest of the Eastern Hemisphere. It also controls the Suez Canal, the shortest sea link between the Indian Ocean and the Mediterranean Sea. Most people in this country live along the Nile River or the Suez Canal. About two-thirds of the country is covered by the Libyan Desert. This desert is part of the Sahara and is mostly a sandy plateau. The Arabian or Eastern Desert is also a part of the Sahara and spreads to the east of the Nile River. The Sinai Peninsula is mostly a desert region located east of the Suez Canal and the Gulf of Suez. The peninsula has rich oil deposits.

More than half of the country's citizens live in cities. This causes some of the same problems as other major world cities—crowding and congested streets. There are both wealthy and poor people in the cities. The poor often live in shacks built on other people's land or on the roofs of buildings. Fellahin, or farmers, make up the other half of the population and they mostly live on small pieces of land where they farm or tend animals. A few people are Bedouin nomads who herd animals in the deserts.

This country was once self-sufficient in food supply, but today it imports nearly one-half of its food. It is one of the largest exporters of cotton in the world. Corn, sugarcane, wheat, rice, figs, mangoes, dates, and grapes are the main crops.

There are many important sites to see in this country. The Great Sphinx, a huge statue made of limestone and shaped like a lion with a human head, is 240 ft. (73 m) long and 66 ft. (20 m) high and was built approximately 4,500 years ago. The Aswan High Dam began operating in 1968 and has allowed more than two million acres of land to be farmed. The Valley of the Kings is a gorge that was used as a burial ground between 1550 B.C. and 1100 B.C. by pharaohs of this country. There are also numerous pyramids, built in ancient times, that are tourist attractions.

Where in the world are you?

Political Map of Egypt

Directions: Use the map below to answer the questions. Circle the correct answers.

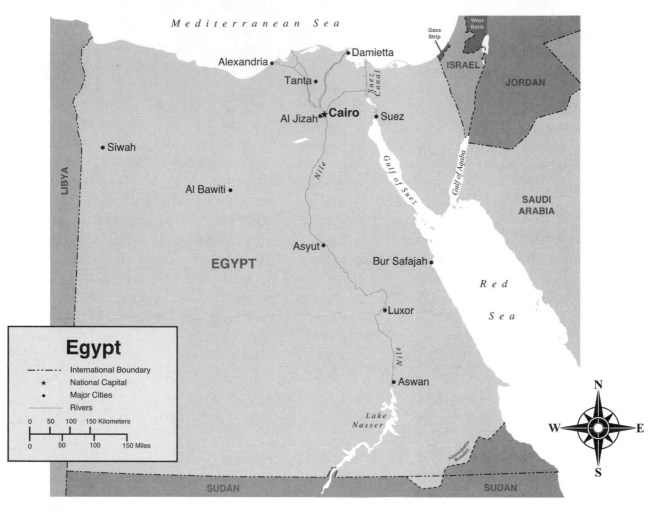

1. The country of Egypt is bordered on the south by _____.
   a. Libya   b. Red Sea   c. Sudan   d. Mediterranean Sea

2. The distance between Cairo and _____ is approximately 200 miles.
   a. Suez   b. Aswan   c. Luxor   d. Asyut

3. The city of _____ lies along the Mediterranean Sea coast.
   a. Alexandria   b. Bur Safajah   c. Tanta   d. Siwah

4. The capital city of Egypt is _____.
   a. Al Jizah   b. Cairo   c. Damietta   d. Suez

5. The Suez Canal lies to the _____ of Lake Nasser.
   a. north   b. south   c. east   d. west

Egyptian Puzzle

Directions: Complete the puzzle using the clues below.

Across

3. A large city in Egypt
4. It was built to help farm more than two million acres of land
7. Gorge used as a cemetery
12. Capital city of Egypt
13. Egyptian farmers

Down

1. Highest mountain in Egypt
2. Statue with the body of a lion and the head of a man
5. Provides a sea link between the Mediterranean and the Indian Ocean
6. Egyptian basic currency
8. The main language in Egypt
9. River that runs through Egypt
10. Peninsula to the east of the Suez Canal
11. Country that borders Egypt to the west
14. Egypt's main religion

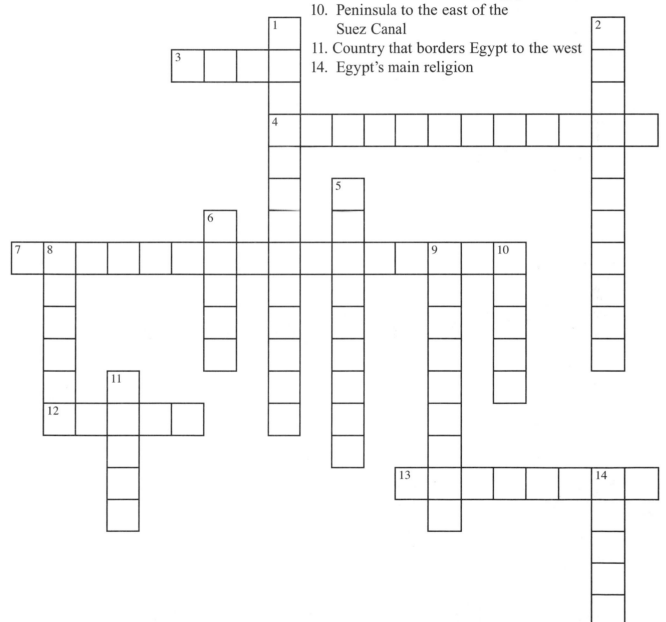

CD-4347 • World Geography

Where in the World Are You?

Capital: Abuja

Largest Cities: Lagos, Ibadan, Kano

Population: 133,881,702 (July 2003 Est.)

Land Area: 351,649 sq. mi. (910,768 sq km)

Highest Mountain: Chappal Waddi (7936 ft./ 2,419 m)

Main Languages: English, Hausa, Yoruba, Igbo

Ethnic Groups: Hausa, Yoruba, Igbo

Main Religions: Muslim, Christian

Government: Republic in transition from military to civilian rule

Basic Currency: Naira

The flag consists of three vertical stripes of green, white, and green.

This is the most populous country in Africa. There are more than 250 ethnic groups. The country ranks tenth in the world in population. It measures more than 650 mi. (1,046 km) from north to south and 800 mi. (1,287 km) from east to west. It is more than twice the size of California in the United States. The coastline is about 478 miles (769 km) long. There are many different landforms including swamps, plains, tropical forests, hills, and mountains. Africa's third longest river, Niger, is located in this country. The Niger is about 2,600 mi. (4,180 km) long. The country is bordered on the north by Niger, to the east by Chad and Cameroon, to the south by the Gulf of Guinea, and to the west by Benin.

Approximately half of the people here live in cities. This is a big change within the last ten to twelve years. Fifteen to twenty percent of the population live in just two cities, Lagos and Ibadan. In the cities, the wealthy live in modern apartments, and the poor sometimes live in slums. Some urban dwellers wear Western-style clothing, but some city dwellers and many of the people who live in rural areas wear traditional clothing.

Some of the sports enjoyed in this country are soccer, polo, cricket, swimming, and wrestling. Children and adults also enjoy a game that is popular all over Africa. The game has different names. In this country it is called the ayo game. This game is played on a board that looks like an open egg carton. It usually has 12-14 sections but could have as many as 60. The game is played by two people using any of a variety of round objects, such as seeds, stones, or marbles.

There are numerous celebrations that take place. One such festival, durbar, is a Muslim celebration that takes place twice a year in the north. The festival combines a display of horsemanship and a display of wealth. Another festival, Argungu Fishing Festival, is celebrated in the northwest along the Sokoto River. Fishermen jump into the river with butterfly nets and calabashes, dried gourds, to scoop up fish.

This country is one of the world's leaders in oil exportation. They also are important miners of limestone, marble, tin and coal. The main agricultural products are beans, beef, cacao, cassava, and corn.

Where in the world are you?

Political Map of Nigeria

Directions: Use the map of Nigeria to answer the questions. Circle the correct answers.

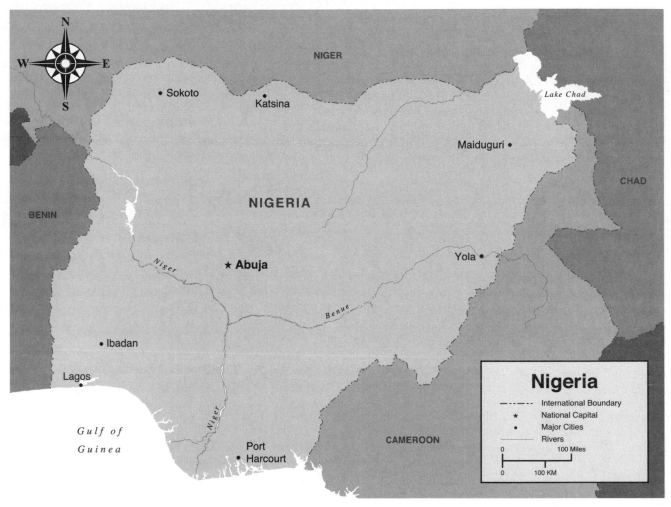

1. The Benue River joins the Niger River south of the city of _____.
   a. Port Harcourt   b. Ibadan   c. Abuja   d. Lagos

2. The city of _____ is located along the Benue River.
   a. Ibadan   b. Yola   c. Port Harcourt   d. Katsina

3. The distance from Abuja to Ibadan is approximately _____.
   a. 100 miles   b. 200 kilometers   c. 100 kilometers   d. 200 miles

4. The country of _____ borders Nigeria to the west.
   a. Niger   b. Cameroon   c. Benin   d. Mali

5. The city of Ibadan is located northeast of the city of _____.
   a. Lagos   b. Yola   c. Sokoto   d. Katsina

Making an African Mask

In many parts of Africa, masks are a very important part of their culture. The masks can be very elaborate and decorative. Each mask has its own purpose. Some may be worn as ornaments while others are used in religious ceremonies. Each tribe has its own unique masks that are made from different materials. Some masks may be carved from wood. Others utilize natural materials such as grass, animal hides, or shells. The masks are usually decorated with simple, strong, and powerful shapes as well as designs. Many of the masks are painted with symbolic designs and colors.

In Nigeria, members of the Igbo (Ibo) tribe express their feelings by means of masks and headdresses: the male symbolizes the elephant, most powerful of all bush creatures; the female symbolizes culture and is delicately coifed to express refinement and civilization. The mask-makers in Zambia combine bark and mud to create ferocious faces that they paint in such colors as red, black, and white.

Now, it is your turn to make an African ceremonial mask, using the suggested materials and directions.

Materials:

1 sheet of white tagboard
colored markers
construction paper
stapler
hole punch
assorted colors of yarn

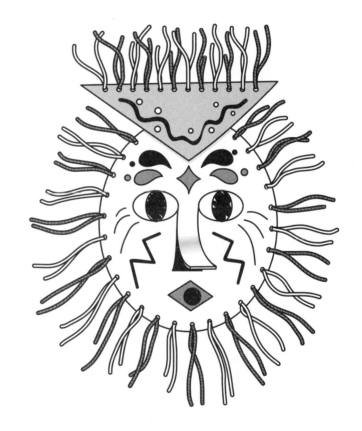

Directions:

1. First, cut a ten-inch (27 cm) piece of tagboard in an oval for your mask.
2. Then, sketch a face or design on the oval tagboard.
3. Using colored marking pens, color the tagboard.
4. Cut around the nose and then bend forward.
5. Next, cut a geometric shape. Staple the geometric shape to the top of the oval shape face.
6. Then, use a hole punch to make holes all around the edges of the face.
7. Finally, take assorted colors of yarn, lace them through individual holes, and tie them securely to add the finishing touches to your ceremonial mask.

Where in the World Are You?

Capitals: Pretoria (administrative), Cape Town (legislative), Bloemfontein (judicial)

Largest Cities: Durban, Cape Town, Johannesburg

Population: 43,586,097 (July 2003 Est.)

Land Area: 471,011 sq. mi. (1,219,912 sq km)

Highest Mountain: Njesuthi (11,181 ft./3,408 m)

Main Languages: Afrikaans, English

Ethnic Groups: Black, White

Main Religions: Christian, animist

Government: Republic

Basic Currency: Rand

A green Y on its side divides the flag into black on the left, red on the top, and blue on the bottom. The red and blue sections are trimmed in white. The black section is trimmed in gold.

This country is located at the southernmost tip of the continent of Africa. It borders six others, including Botswana and Zimbabwe to the north, Namibia to the northwest, Swaziland to the northeast, and Mozambique on the east. The tiny country of Lesotho is surrounded by this country. The distance from north to south is about 875 mi. (1,408 km) and 1,010 mi. (1,625 km) from east to west. The coastline stretches about 1,650 mi. (2,655 km) on the Indian and South Atlantic Oceans.

There is a wide variety of landforms in the country. They include mountains, a plateau, a coastal strip, and two deserts, the Namib and the Kalahari. Differences in elevation, wind systems, and ocean currents have varying effects on the climate. Only a fourth of the country receives more than 25 inches (64 cm) of rain annually. The coastal strip has dry, sunny winters and hot, humid summers. The Cape Mountains have cool, wet winters and warm, dry summers.

Even though the country takes up just 4% of the continent's land and has only 6% of the people, it has 40% of the industrial production and 25% of the continent's wealth. The main industries include mining, steel, chemicals, and vehicles. The chief crops are corn, wheat, vegetables, sugar, and fruit. This country is the world's leader in the production of gold. It has 40% of the world's gold reserves, more than 75% of the platinum and almost 75% of the chromium reserves.

Rugby and soccer are important sports in this country. The Cape to Rio yacht race is held every three years. The race begins in Cape Town and ends in Rio de Janeiro, Brazil. This race is treacherous and lasts for three to four weeks. Music and dance are important and are enjoyed by many people in the country. One of the most famous choral singing groups is Ladysmith Black Mombazo. The choral singing is without musical accompaniment. One dance that is well-known in the country is the Zulu foot-stomping gumboot.

Mealie pap is a kind of porridge made from maize (corn) flour. Biltong is another favorite food. Biltong is similar to beef jerky but said to be tastier. Biltong can be made with any type of meat and in this country that might be ostrich.

Where in the world are you?

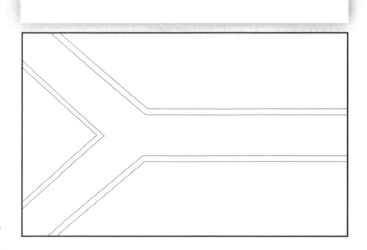

Political Map of South Africa

Directions: Use the map below to answer the questions. Circle the correct answers.

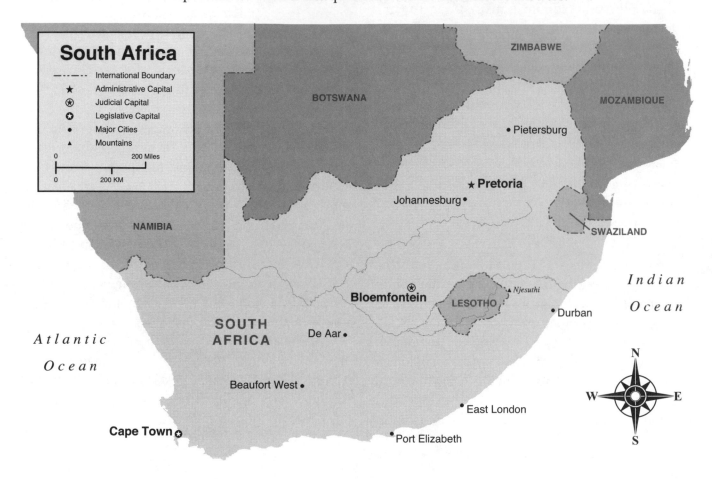

1. The city of _____ is located on the east coast bordered by the Indian Ocean.
       a. De Aar   b. Beaufort West   c. Durban   d. Pretoria

2. The distance between Port Elizabeth and East London is less than _____.
       a. 100 kilometers   b. 50 kilometers   c. 100 miles   d. 200 miles

3. The city of _____ is located on the southwestern coast.
       a. Pietersburg   b. Pretoria   c. East London   d. Cape Town

4. Bloemfontein is approximately 500 kilometers west of _____.
       a. Pietersburg   b. Durban   c. Port Elisabeth   d. De Aar

5. Njesuthi is located near the border of _____.
       a. Lesotho   b. Namibia   c. Zimbabwe   d. Swaziland

South Africa Word Search

Directions: Locate and circle the words listed below in the South Africa word search.

```
N U M N P X H X S E U N P D A N P F L
T W A I D E G H G Z M B T U I C A V O L
S R O E N N Y G Z W H A R R A P Q Y O O
Y B E T T I A O I K E B O P E H A Y T O
C Z Z S E A N R Q H A T E I R O U T S J
C R O J E P L G W N E M L Q Y Q O R T N
M M J Z C D A P R R O A I P E U F E O I
D I S N G U I C P U E V Q H F M R S M E
X N Q R J Y E R N M U R N G S P Z E P T
F S S G M E B T A P R B B A I B F D I N
F G X D Y I A C A H L E K T W O Y B N O
O M L B L I H B P G A A P M N K Y I G F
X O G T N R Q J L P U L T U H Y F M Q M
G U O S O R L F P W H W A I B L C A D E
R N M M A O W T U D G Q I K N L E N R O
G Y I C I S F F F O I N L R K U I E P L
G U Y A C H T R A C I N G H F N M C T B
M J O H A N N E S B U R G B N A R F H S
M S U N T N J E S U T H I D P P O O W A
P P J A N G N I G N I S L A R O H C C V
```

JOHANNESBURG	RUGBY	PRETORIA
NAMIB DESERT	CAPE MOUNTAINS	WHEAT
REPUBLIC	DURBAN	CHORAL SINGING
BILTONG	MEALIE PAP	GOLD
BLOEMFONTEIN	PLATINUM	NJESUTHI
CORN	STEEL	RAND
KALAHARI DESERT	CAPE TOWN	YACHT RACING
PLATEAU	FOOT STOMPING	CHROMIUM
	MINING	

Where in the World Are You?

Capital: Khartoum

Largest Cities: Omdurman, Khartoum North, Port Sudan

Population: 38,114,160 (July 2003 Est.)

Land Area: 967,494 sq. mi. (2,376,000 sq km)

Highest Mountain: Mt. Kinyeti (10,456 ft./3,187 m)

Main Languages: Arabic, English, Tribal Languages

Ethnic Groups: Arab-African, Black African

Main Religions: Sunni Muslim, Indigenous beliefs, Christian

Government: Authoritarian regime

Basic Currency: Dinar

The flag consists of horizontal stripes of red, white, and black with a green triangle on the left side.

This country is the largest country in size in Africa. It is about one third the size of the United States The country measures approximately 1,275 mi. (2,050 km) from north to south and 1,150 mi. (1,850 km) from east to west. It has about 400 mi. (644 km) of coastline along the Red Sea. Egypt borders the country to the north; Libya, Chad, and the Central African Republic to the west; Democratic Republic of the Congo, Uganda, and Kenya to the south; and Ethiopia, Eritrea, and the Red Sea to the east.

The country has four geographical regions. In the north there are deserts, both the Libyan and Nubian, which cover about 30% of the country's land area. To the south of the desert is a semi-arid region consisting of grassland and low hills which cover most of the central part of the country. Farther to the south is a swampy area called the Sudd. In the farthest southern area is the rain forest. The Blue Nile enters the country from Ethiopia and the White Nile comes in from Uganda. They meet together in the city of Khartoum and form the Nile, which flows north through the rest of country.

The lives and clothing of the people here vary greatly from north to south. In the north, there is a strong Islamic influence. Farther south, people live more traditionally, depending on their ethnic groups. About four-fifths of the people live in rural areas and the remaining fifth live in urban areas. The people in rural areas mainly raise livestock or farm by traditional methods. Both modern and traditional clothing may be seen.

Some traditional foods served here include ful, a dish made of cooked beans often served with raw onions. They also eat a type of flat unleavened bread made from sorghum called kisra. The first meal of the day is sometimes a dish with liver, such as cooked liver with ful and fish, or raw lungs and liver served with hot chili. For feasts the menu might include maschi, tomatoes and eggplant stuffed with rice and minced lamb; gammonia, stewed sheep's stomach, served with onions and tomatoes; and kisra, fresh fruit segments.

Where in the world are you?

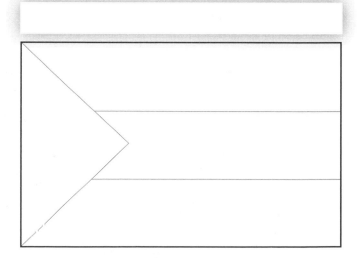

Political Map of Sudan

Directions: Use the map of Sudan to answer the following questions. Circle the correct answers.

1. The capital city of Sudan is _____.
   a. Waw
   b. Bor
   c. Port Sudan
   d. Khartoum

2. All of the following cities are located along the Nile except _____.
   a. Juba   b. Al Fashir
   c. Atbara   d. Kusti

3. The city of _____ is located along the border between Sudan and Uganda.
   a. Al Fashir
   b. Waw
   c. Nimule
   d. Port Sudan

4. Khartoum is located farther north than the city of _____.
   a. Wadi Halfa
   b. Kusti
   c. Port Sudan
   d. Atbara

5. The distance from Atbara to Port Sudan is approximately _____.
   a. 50 miles
   b. 125 miles
   c. 450 kilometers
   d. 250 kilometers

6. _____ is located on the coastline of the Red Sea.
   a. Atbara   b. Nimule
   c. Juba   d. Port Sudan

Sudan

- - - - - International Boundary
★ National Capital
• Major Cities
—— Rivers

0 _____ 250 Miles
0 _____ 250 KM

SAUDI ARABIA

EGYPT

LIBYA

Red Sea

Wadi Halfa •

Disputed Border

Port Sudan •

Nile

CHAD

• Atbara

Khartoum ★

ERITREA

• Al Fashir

Kusti •

Blue Nile

White Nile

SUDAN

ETHIOPIA

Waw •

CENTRAL AFRICAN REPUBLIC

• Juba

Disputed Border

• Nimule

DEM. REP. OF CONGO

UGANDA

KENYA

Sudan Scramble

Directions: Unscramble the following words by placing the letters in the blanks provided. Use the numbered letters to solve the second puzzle.

ODNMURAM   _ _ _ _ _ _ _ _
                3   26

AARCBI   _ _ _ _ _ _
         13   36

ISAML   _ _ _ _ _
          11

LNBAYI EDSTRE   _ _ _ _ _ _ _ _ _ _
                   12   10   17

NUAINB TDSREE   _ _ _ _ _ _ _ _ _ _
         20   25 32   22

DSUD   _ _ _ _
     16

BULE LEIN   _ _ _ _ _ _ _ _
               21 6   29

HOKMTRAU   _ _ _ _ _ _ _ _
       9 37 34

FLU   _ _ _
   33 2

IRKSA   _ _ _ _ _
     28 1 23

GAIMANMO   _ _ _ _ _ _ _ _
    14   30 4

ACHMIS   _ _ _ _ _ _
     7 18

TOPR ADSNU   _ _ _ _ _ _ _ _ _
         8   27   5

MNTOU KYEIITN   _ _ _ _ _ _ _ _ _ _ _
     19   31 24 15   35

_ _ _ _ _   _ _   _ _ _   _ _ _ _ _ _   _ _ _ _ _ _ _ _ _
1 2 3 4 5   6 7   8 9 10   11 12 13 14 15 16 17   18 19 20 21 22 23 24   25 26

_ _ Z _   _ _   _ _ _ _ _ _ _.
27 28   29   30 31   32 33 34 35 36 37

CD-4347 • World Geography

Capital: Nairobi

Largest Cities: Nairobi, Mombasa, Kisumu

Population: 31,639,091 (July 2003 Est.)

Land Area: 219,789 sq. mi. (569,250 sq km)

Highest Mountain: Mt. Kenya (17,058 ft./5,199 m)

Main Languages: English, Swahili, other African languages

Ethnic Groups: Kikuyu, Luhya, Luo, Kalenjin, Kamba, other African groups

Main Religions: Protestant, Roman Catholic

Government: Republic

Basic Currency: Shilling

The flag consists of three horizontal stripes of black, red, and green divided by narrow white stripes. A shield and two spears are centered on the flag.

This country has snow-covered mountain peaks, sandy beaches, savannas, fertile fields, orchards, and vast deserts. The wildlife includes elephants, water buffalo, giraffes, lions, and baboons. These animals are protected in the country's many national parks and game preserves. The country is located in eastern Africa and is divided almost in half by the equator. It is a little larger than France and a little smaller than Texas in the United States. It borders Tanzania, Uganda, Sudan, Ethiopia, Somalia, and the Indian Ocean. A major physical feature of the country is the Great Rift Valley. The valley is a huge crack that is more than 4,500 mi. (7,200 km) long and extends from southwest Asia down through most of east Africa. The Great Rift Valley is marked with volcanoes and a chain of seven lakes. On each side of the valley, walls rise to heights that range from 100 ft. (30 m) to more than 4,000 ft. (1,200 m).

Even though only one-fifth of the land is suitable for farming, about 70% of the workers are engaged in farming. Coffee, corn, and tea are the chief crops produced in this country. Gold, limestone, salt, rubies, and fluorspar are the main minerals. Cattle, chickens, and goats are the main types of livestock.

The economy is dependent upon agriculture, manufacturing, commerce, and tourism.

National sports include soccer and track and field events. Rugby, cricket, and volleyball are played in many colleges, schools, and clubs. There are more than 20 sports clubs in the city of Nairobi alone. Many of this country's runners have held world records. Almost all of the athletic stars from this country have come from the Great Rift Valley region.

Storytelling, dance, and music are important parts of the culture. School children learn to sing and recite traditional songs and stories and often perform for a variety of occasions. Nairobi has its own symphony orchestra and theater company. Choirs are also an important part of the culture. The Mungano National Choir has made numerous recordings and performed in various countries around the world. Many movies have been filmed in the country, including *Out of Africa*. These films have helped to boost the country's tourist industry.

Where in the world are you?

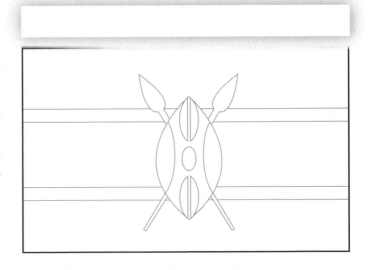

Political Map of Kenya

Directions: Use the map of Kenya to answer the following questions. Circle the correct answers.

1. The _____ forms the southeastern boundary of Kenya.
   a. Uganda
   b. Ethiopia
   c. Indian Ocean
   d. Lake Victoria

2. In northwest Kenya, you can visit _____.
   a. Wajir
   b. Lake Rudolf
   c. Mombasa
   d. Lake Victoria

3. The distance between Mado Gashi and Wajir is approximately _____.
   a. 50 kilometers
   b. 50 miles
   c. 100 miles
   d. 300 kilometers

4. The capital of Kenya is _____.
   a. Nairobi   b. Nakuru
   c. Lamu   d. Mombasa

5. The Great Rift Valley is found in _____ Kenya.
   a. northern
   b. southern
   c. eastern
   d. western

6. All of these cities are located on Kenya's coast except _____.
   a. Lamu   b. Malindi
   c. Mombasa   d. Moyale

SUDAN

ETHIOPIA

Lake Rudolf (Lake Turkana)

Moyale

UGANDA

Great Rift Valley

KENYA

Wajir

SOMALIA

Mado Gashi

Mt. Kenya

Nakuru

Lake Victoria

Nairobi ★

Lamu

TANZANIA

Malindi

Indian Ocean

Mombasa

Kenya

- - - - International Boundary
★ National Capital
• Major Cities
▲ Mountains

0   50   100 Kilometers
0   50   100 Miles

N
W   E
S

Kenya Animal Scramble

Kenya is world famous for its animal wildlife. The country's plains and its highlands are the home to large numbers of animals. Tourists come to Kenya to see wildlife. Kenya has large national parks owned by the government where wild animals are protected. Tourists can drive through the parks to watch and to photograph wildlife.

Directions: Unscramble the letters below to form the name of the animal or bird. Write the answers on the spaces provided.

1. NPEALHAET   _ _ _ _ _ _ _ _

2. FREGFAI   _ _ _ _ _ _ _

3. CNREHRIOSO   _ _ _ _ _ _ _ _ _

4. REBAZ   _ _ _ _ _

5. THSIOCR   _ _ _ _ _ _ _

6. NOIL   _ _ _ _

7. HTEHCEA   _ _ _ _ _ _ _

8. LTEAPNOE   _ _ _ _ _ _ _ _

9. DRAPOEL   _ _ _ _ _ _ _

10. OFΛBLFU   _ _ _ _ _ _ _

11. MIOSPAPTHOPU   _ _ _ _ _ _ _ _ _ _ _ _

12. LAEGE   _ _ _ _ _

13. GOHTRAW   _ _ _ _ _ _ _

14. TRSKO   _ _ _ _ _

Compare and Contrast Selected African Countries

Directions: Use the following information to answer the questions below. Circle the correct answers.

Country	Area (square km)	Population Density (per square km 1997)	Life Expectancy at Birth (1990-1999)		Largest Export Industries (% of exports, 1998)
			Female	Male	
Egypt	1,001,449	62	68	65	Chemicals 34% Textiles 21% Mining, Quarry 19%
Kenya	580,367	57	53	51	Agriculture 50% Chemicals 18% Food, Beverage, Tobacco 13%
Morocco	446,550	61	69	65	Chemicals 24% Agriculture 22% Textiles 21%
Nigeria	923,768	128	52	49	No Data Available
South Africa	1,221,037	35	58	52	Mining, Quarry 26% Metal manufacturing 20% Other Manufacturing 13%
Sudan	2,505,813	11	56	54	Agriculture 71% Food, Beverage, Tobacco 21% Textiles 8%

1. Chemicals are among the leading export industries in _____ of these African countries.
   a. two   b. three   c. four   d. five

2. Life expectancy for males in South Africa is the same as females in _____.
   a. Egypt   b. Sudan   c. Kenya   d. Nigeria

3. There are about twice as many people per square mile in Nigeria as there are in _____.
   a. South Africa   b. Sudan   c. Kenya   d. Egypt

4. Sudan has about one and a half million more people than _____.
   a. Kenya   b. Egypt   c. Morocco   d. Nigeria

5. The countries of Egypt and Morocco export about _____ % textiles.
   a. 34   b. 8   c. 21   d. 13

Physical Geography of Antarctica

Location:

Located almost entirely within the Antarctic Circle and totally in the southern hemisphere, Antarctica surrounds the South Pole. This pole is the southernmost place on Earth. The continent is bordered by the Atlantic Ocean, the Indian Ocean, and the Pacific Ocean. Approximately 500 million years ago, Antarctica was located at the equator. As the continent drifted, Antarctica moved south. During the time of the dinosaurs, it was attached to Australia. It continued to drift farther south and separated from Australia.

Area:

Antarctica is about 5,400,000 sq. mi. (14,000,000 sq km) in size. This continent is about one and one-half times larger than the United States. Approximately 2% of the continent is ice-free; the other portion is ice-covered. Antarctica is the fifth largest continent. It measures approximately 1,616 miles (2,600 km) at its greatest distance and about 2,734 miles (4,400 km) at its shortest distance. The highest point on the continent, Vinson Massif, is 16,864 feet (5,140 m) above sea level.

Landforms:

Approximately 98% of the land is covered with a thick, continental ice sheet. In some places the ice is approximately 14,000 feet (4,270 m) thick. About 70% of the world's fresh water is contained within the continent's ice. Most of Ross Sea and Weddell Sea are covered by ice shelves. An ice shelf is a permanent ice formation that extends over the sea. Several of these have formed in the coastal areas of Antarctica. The continent is surrounded by water and covered by permafrost, permanently frozen ground. The continent contains the world's largest cold desert.

There are no lakes or rivers on Antarctica because of the extreme cold temperatures. It does have huge glaciers, moving masses of ice.

The Transantarctic Mountains are the main mountain range on the continent. They stretch across the entire continent from the Ross Sea in the west to the tip of the Antarctic Peninsula. The highest peak in the chain is Vinson Massif. The average elevation on the continent is between 6,562-13,123 ft. (2,000-4,000 m).

Climate:

The coldest, windiest, and driest place on Earth is the South Pole. The coldest temperature ever recorded on earth was at the South Pole where the temperature reached –128.6° F (-88° C). Most of Antarctica receives less than two inches of snow each year. During spring and summer (mid-September to mid-March), they experience continuous sunlight and continuous darkness in fall and winter (mid-March to mid-September).

People and Animals:

Even though scientific expeditions travel to Antarctica, there are no native human residents. Due to the extreme weather, scientists do not stay there year-round. The seas around Antarctica are filled with life, ranging from the huge blue whale to tiny plankton.

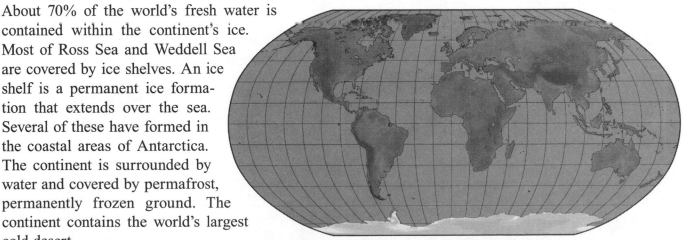

Physical Map of Antarctica

Directions: Use the map of Antarctica to answer the questions. Circle the correct answers.

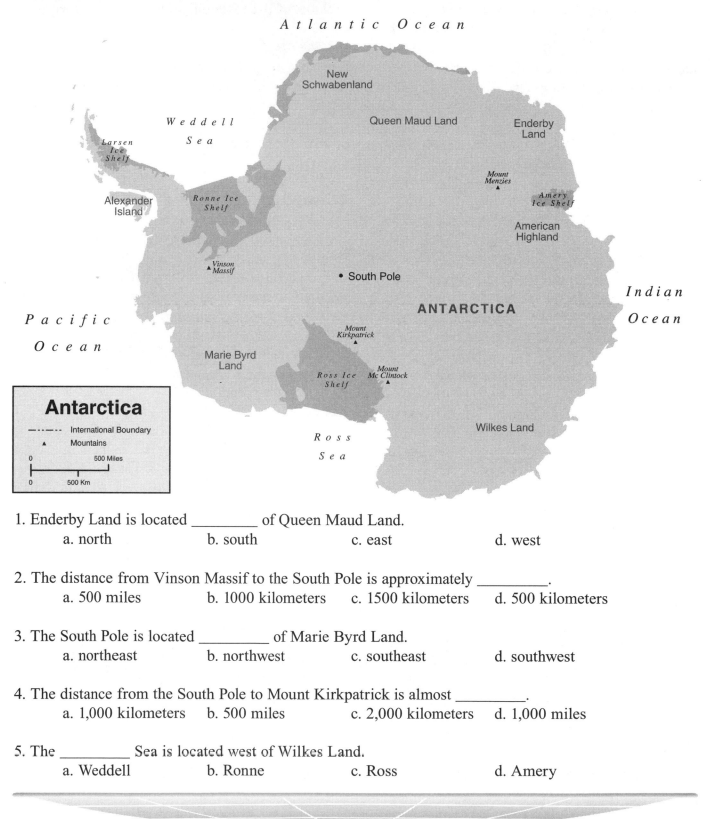

1. Enderby Land is located _____ of Queen Maud Land.
   - a. north
   - b. south
   - c. east
   - d. west

2. The distance from Vinson Massif to the South Pole is approximately _____.
   - a. 500 miles
   - b. 1000 kilometers
   - c. 1500 kilometers
   - d. 500 kilometers

3. The South Pole is located _____ of Marie Byrd Land.
   - a. northeast
   - b. northwest
   - c. southeast
   - d. southwest

4. The distance from the South Pole to Mount Kirkpatrick is almost _____.
   - a. 1,000 kilometers
   - b. 500 miles
   - c. 2,000 kilometers
   - d. 1,000 miles

5. The _____ Sea is located west of Wilkes Land.
   - a. Weddell
   - b. Ronne
   - c. Ross
   - d. Amery

Political Map of Antarctica

Research stations are maintained on the continent of Antarctica by many countries. Scientists conduct research in many areas at their assigned stations. Most research teams stay only during the summer months; however, others stay throughout the year.

Directions: Study the map which shows the research stations and the sponsoring countries; then answer the questions.

Maitri (India)
Sanae (S. Afr.)
Syowa (Japan)
Bellinghausen (Russia)
Weddell Sea
Halley (U.K.)
Palmer (U.S.)
Larsen Ice Shelf
Mawson (Aus.)
Belgrano (Arg.)
Rothera (U.K.)
Ronne Ice Shelf
ANTARCTICA
Amery Ice Shelf
Davis (Aus.)
South Pole
Amundsen-Scott (U.S.)
Indian Ocean
Pacific Ocean
Vostok (Russia)
Ross Ice Shelf
Casey (Aus.)
Scott (N.Z.) • McMurdo (U.S.)
Ross Sea
Dumont d'Urville (France)

Antarctica
- - - - - International Boundary
• Research Stations
0   1000 Miles
0   1000 Km

1. The Sanae Station is sponsored by the country of _____.
    a. India   b. South Africa   c. Russia   d. United States

2. The _____ Station, sponsored by the United States, is located near the South Pole.
    a. Vostok   b. Davis   c. Palmer   d. Amundsen-Scott

3. The United Kingdom sponsors the _____ station.
    a. Palmer   b. Casey   c. Dumont d'Urville   d. Halley

4. At this time, Australia sponsors _____ research stations in Antarctica.
    a. three   b. four   c. five   d. six

5. All of the following countries have research stations in Antarctica except _____.
    a. Argentina   b. India   c. Canada   d. France

Scrambling through Antarctica

Directions: Unscramble the following words by placing the letters in the blanks provided. Use the numbered letters to solve the second puzzle.

1. INACTRTAC CIRELC _ _ _ _ _ _ _ _   _ _ _ _ _ _
                          9   43 37

2. LOTAPNKN _ _ _ _ _ _ _ _
                17   12

3. TNTSSEIISC _ _ _ _ _ _ _ _ _ _
               11   33 41

4. WSEILK NLDA _ _ _ _ _ _   _ _ _ _
                16   26

5. OHSUT PEOL _ _ _ _ _   _ _ _ _
              27 36 3   23

6. NVSINO FMSSAI _ _ _ _ _ _   _ _ _ _ _
                    2   1

7. GEALRICS _ _ _ _ _ _ _ _
             31 25 4 35

8. NLOTNCNAIET CIE EHSET _ _ _ _ _ _ _ _ _ _ _   _ _ _   _ _ _ _ _
                            7   34 29   21   44

9. BLEU WLEHA _ _ _ _   _ _ _ _ _
                        22 10

10. RSOS SAE _ _ _ _   _ _ _
              5   40

11. PREORFMTAS _ _ _ _ _ _ _ _ _ _
                32 24   18 14

12. WELDDEL SAE _ _ _ _ _ _ _   _ _ _
                 42 38 39   15

13. EIC FHLES _ _ _   _ _ _ _ _
                6   20

14. AAITTCRNC NIPNLUSAE _ _ _ _ _ _ _ _ _   _ _ _ _ _ _ _ _ _
                          19   30   13 8   28

_ _ _ _ _ _ _ _ _ _   _ _ _ _ _ _ _ _   _ _ _ _ _ _ _ ,
1 2 3 4 5 6 7 8 9 10 11 12 13 14 15 16 17 18 19 20 21 22 23 24 25 26 27

_ _ _ _ _ _ _   _ _ _ _ _ _ _ _ _ _ .
28 29 30 31 32 33 34 35 36 37 38 39 40 41 42 43 44

You Are a Travel Agent!

Imagine that you are a travel agent! The Cortez's, a very wealthy couple from Brazil, wants to make a trip to at least six of the seven continents. They want to visit as many countries, cities, landmarks, and special places of interest during their trip around the world in six weeks. Before beginning their itinerary, you may want to use extra paper to start planning their six-week trip to six continents. Use the space below for your final itinerary.

Itinerary	
Week 1	Week 2
Week 3	Week 4
Week 5	Week 6

World Geography: Web Sites

Geographia

http://www.geographia.com

Well-written articles on Africa, Asia, the Caribbean, Europe, and Latin America are featured on this site.

Geography Education From National Geographic

http://www.nationalgeographic.com

http://www.nationalgeographic.com/resources/ngo/education/

Many lesson plans and classroom ideas are included here. Also featured are a geography discussion forum, maps, and information on the geography bee.

Map Machine (National Geographic)

http://www.nationalgeographic.com/resources/ngo/maps/

With excellent maps of the world and individual countries, this site also offers flag images, cartographic information, facts, and profiles of the countries of the world as well as the United States.

National Oceanic and Atmospheric Administration

http://www.noaa.gov

http://www.education.noaa.gov

The education site of the National Oceanic and Atmospheric Administration (NOAA) is an excellent resource for students and teachers in grades K-12. This site provides booklets, activities, publications, and reference material for classroom use.

United Nations

http://un.org

This site includes a section on maps and is offered in various languages, including Spanish and French. It also features http://cyberschoolbus.un.org, an educational site providing overviews of individual countries and educational games involving country flags.

Virtual Field Trips

http://www.field-guides.com

Field trips without permission slips; what a concept! At this site you can travel to different parts of the world and experience different natural phenomena. Categories include: Deserts, Hurricanes, Natural Wonders, Sharks, Tornadoes, and much more.

The World Factbook

http://www.odci.gov/cia/publications/factbook/

The World Factbook is one of the premier reference resources on the Web. The Central Intelligence Agency has compiled a wealth of information on countries from Afghanistan to Zimbabwe.

Glossary of Geographic Terms

Agriculture: using lands for keeping and grazing animals or growing crops

Archipelago: group or chain of islands

Arid: dry

Atoll: small reefs or islands that form a ring around a shallow pool of water

Bay: part of a sea that is smaller than a gulf and partly surrounded by land

Canal: an inland waterway built to carry water for irrigation or transportation

Canyon: deep valley with steep sides and a stream running through it

Coast: land along the sea

Communism: political system of government in which land, industry, and property are controlled by the government or state for equal use by all citizens

Dam: a piece of land or a structure that is used to hold back the flow of a body of water

Deforestation: loss of areas of forest due to human consumption

Democracy: system of government where the people elect those who govern them

Desert: a dry region where more water is lost due to evaporation than falls as precipitation

Desertification: the spread of a desert due to climate change or mismanagement

Drought: long period of dry weather, possibly leading to a dangerous shortage of water

Economy: the way a country produces, uses, and distributes its money, resources, goods, and services

Equator: imaginary line around the middle of the earth at an equal distance from the North and South Poles—zero degrees latitude

Erosion: the gradual wearing or washing away of rock, land, or buildings by the forces of wind and water

Ethnic Group: group of people within a larger community who have common characteristics such as language, religion, or customs

Export: product made in one country and sold to another

Glacier: a large sheet of ice that moves slowly over some land surface or down a valley

Globe: a spherical model representing Earth as it looks from space

Grid: the system of latitude and longitude lines that helps find places on a map

Gross National Product (GNP): the per-person figure that represents the total value of all goods and services produced in a country in one year

Harbor: a deep body of water where ships can anchor

Hill: a rounded, raised landform, not as high as a mountain

Import: product that is brought into a country from another country

Irrigation: a system for providing a supply of water to crops

Island: body of land completely surrounded by water

Isthmus: a narrow strip of land bordered by water that connects two larger bodies of land

Lagoon: a shallow body of water partly or completely enclosed within an atoll; a shallow body of sea water partly cut off from the sea by a narrow strip of land

Lake: body of water completely surrounded by land

Latitude: horizontal lines measuring distance north and south of the equator

Legend: tells the meanings of the symbols on a map (or map key)

Longitude: vertical lines measuring distance east and west of the prime meridian

Mesa: a high, flat landform rising steeply above the surrounding land—smaller than a plateau, larger than a butte

Monarchy: a system of government in which the land is ruled by a king, queen, emperor, or empress

Glossary of Geographic Terms

Monsoon: extremely strong seasonal wind accompanying wet, stormy weather

Mountain: a high, rounded, or pointed landform with steep sides, higher than a hill

Mouth: the place where a river empties into another body of water

Natural Resource: part of the natural environment that humans can use to satisfy their needs and wants

Oasis: a fertile place in a desert, due to the presence of water

Ocean: one of Earth's four largest bodies of water

Peak: the pointed top of a mountain or hill

Peninsula: a body of land nearly surrounded by water

Plain: a large area of flat or nearly flat land

Plateau: a high, flat landform that rises steeply above the surrounding land—larger than a mesa and a butte

Political Map: a map that shows boundary lines and borders

Population Density: the number of people per unit of land area

Port: a place where ships load and unload goods

Prime Meridian: imaginary line from which longitude is measured both east and west; zero degrees longitude running through Greenwich, England, from the North Pole to the South Pole

Province: area of land that is part of a country or empire

Reef: a ridge of sand, rock, or coral that lies at or near the surface of a sea

Relative Location: identifying where a place is in relationship to other places

Reservoir: a natural or artificial lake used to store water

Region: an area of land that shares one or more common characteristics; can be physical or human characteristics

River: a large stream of water that flows across the land and usually empties into a lake, ocean, or other river

Rural: in, of, or like the country

Scale: shows the measurement of distances and areas

Sea: a large body of water party or entirely surrounded by land; another word for ocean

Strait: a narrow waterway or channel connecting two larger bodies of water

Topography: physical features

Tributary: a river or stream that flows into a larger river or stream

Urban: in, of, or like a city

Valley: an area of lower land between hills or mountains

Volcano: an opening in the earth through which lava, rock, gases, and ash are forced out

Waterfall: a flow of water falling from a high place to a lower place

Wetlands: areas that have wet soils, such as swamps or marshes

Where in the World Are You? Skills Test

Directions: Write the correct letter or letters for the questions below.

_____ 1. Which country is not in Eastern Europe?
        a. Croatia   b. Hungary   c. Belgium   d. Latvia

_____ 2. Which country is not in Asia?
        a. Singapore   b. Greece   c. Thailand   d. Mongolia

_____ 3. Which is not a Central American country?
        a. Guatemala   b. Honduras   c. Costa Rica   d. Uruguay

_____ 4. Which country is the world's largest country in area?
        a. China   b. India   c. Russia   d. Canada

_____ 5. In which hemisphere are Honduras, Costa Rica, Bolivia, Canada and Mexico?
        a. Northern   b. Southern   c. Eastern   d. Western

_____ 6. Which type of climate could not be found along the equator?
        a. polar   b. tropical   c. desert   d. mountain

_____ 7. Which country is farther south in latitude?
        a. Mexico   b. Venezuela   c. South Africa   d. India

_____ 8. Which countries are in the Pacific region?
        a. Fiji   b. Greece   c. South Korea   d. New Zealand

_____ 9. What is the name of the large island off the southeast coast of Africa?
        a. Sicily   b. New Zealand   c. Madagascar   d. Sardinia

_____ 10. Of the following which are Canadian provinces?
        a. Greenland   b. Nova Scotia   c. Ontario   d. Prince Edward Island

Directions: Identify the following geographic locations by using the correct letter on the map.

____ 11. Arctic Ocean
____ 12. Africa
____ 13. Europe
____ 14. Equator
____ 15. Atlantic Ocean
____ 16. Antarctica
____ 17. North America
____ 18. North Pole
____ 19. Indian Ocean
____ 20. Asia
____ 21. South America
____ 22. South Pole
____ 23. Pacific Ocean
____ 24. Australia
____ 25. Prime Meridian

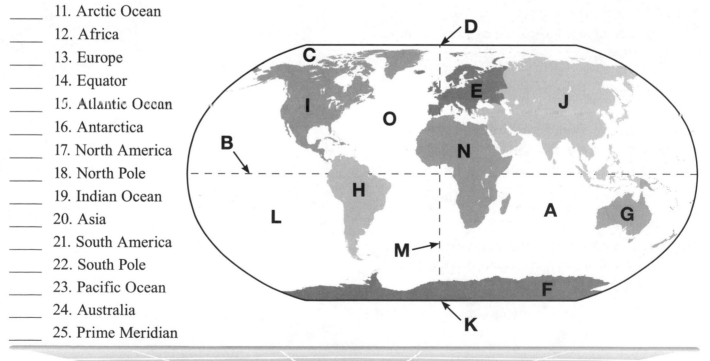

Where in the World Are You? Skills Test

Directions: Write the letter of the geographic feature that matches each definition.

_____ 26. vertical lines measuring distance east and west of the prime meridian

_____ 27. a dry region where more water is lost due to evaporation than falls as precipitation

_____ 28. a narrow waterway or channel connecting two larger bodies of water

_____ 29. a body of land nearly surrounded by water

_____ 30. a group or chain of islands

_____ 31. a river or stream that flows into a larger river or stream

_____ 32. a narrow strip of land, bordered by water, connecting two larger bodies of land

_____ 33. an inland waterway built to carry water for irrigation or transportation

_____ 34. a large, high, flat landform that rises steeply above the surrounding land

_____ 35. physical features

_____ 36. an imaginary line of latitude at 0°

_____ 37. loss of areas of forest due to human consumption

_____ 38. an imaginary line from which longitude is measured both east and west

_____ 39. extremely strong seasonal wind accompanying wet, stormy weather

_____ 40. horizontal lines measuring distance north and south of the equator

A. archipelago	F. isthmus	K. plateau
B. canal	G. latitude	L. prime meridian
C. deforestation	H. longitude	M. strait
D. desert	I. monsoon	N. topography
E. equator	J. peninsula	O. tributary

Directions: Write the correct letter for the "world" matching descriptions below.

_____ 41. longest river in the world   A. Lake Baikal

_____ 42. world's largest desert   B. Saudi Arabia

_____ 43. tallest mountain in the world   C. Lake Superior

_____ 44. largest country in the world   D. Sahara

_____ 45. largest fresh water lake in the world   E. Russia

_____ 46. world's highest navigable lake   F. Nile

_____ 47. deepest lake in the world   G. Lake Titicaca

_____ 48. most populated country on Earth   H. China

_____ 49. largest petroleum deposits in the world   I. Pacific

_____ 50. the world's largest ocean   J. Mount Everest

Answer Key

Page 6
1. L, 2. D, 3. H, 4. C, 5. N, 6. E, 7. M, 8. O, 9. F,
10. K, 11. I, 12. G, 13. A, 14. B, 15. J.

Page 8

Page 11
1. c., 2. a., 3. a., 4. d., 5. b., 6. d.

Page 12

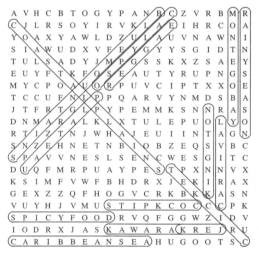

Page 14
1. c., 2. b., 3. a., 4. d., 5. d., 6. b.

Page 15
1. c., 2. b., 3. a., 4. c., 5. d.

Page 17
1. b., 2. d., 3. d., 4. a., 5. c.

Page 18
1. Tajumulco, 2. Quetzal,
3. Guatemala City, 4. Ladino,
5. Cardamom, 6. Soccer,
7. Tropical, 8. Rainy Season,
9. Coffee, 10. Corn,
11. Marimba, 12. School
"Buenos Dias Amigos!"

Page 20
1. b., 2. c., 3. c., 4. b., 5. b.

Page 21

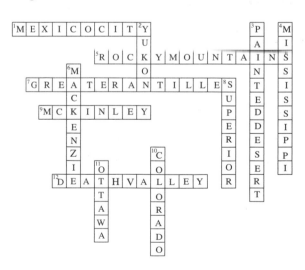

Page 22

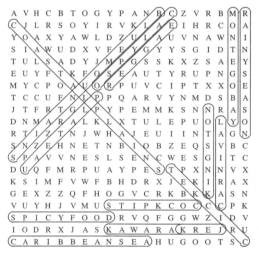

Answer Key

Page 24
1. A., 2 B., 3. K., 4. H., 5. L., 6. G., 7. C., 8. F.,
9. J., 10. D., 11. E., 12. I., 13. M.

Page 26
1. c., 2. b., 3. a., 4. b., 5. d.

Page 27
1. G., 2. I., 3. C., 4. H., 5. A., 6. N., 7. J., 8. O.,
9. M., 10. D., 11. B., 12. L., 13. E., 14. K., 15. F.

Page 29
1. a., 2. c., 3. d., 4. b., 5. a., 6. c., 7. a.

Page 30

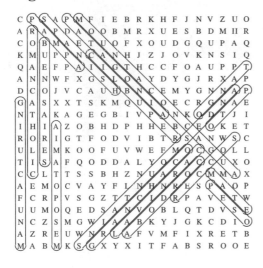

Page 32
1. c., 2. b., 3. d., 4. a., 5. a., 6. b., 7. c., 8. a.

Page 33
1. b., 2. a., 3. a., 4. d., 5. c., 6. c.

Page 35
1. a., 2. b., 3. d., 4. d., 5. b.

Page 36
1. d., 2. b., 3. a., 4. b.

Page 38
1. d., 2. a., 3. b., 4. a., 5. b.

Page 39

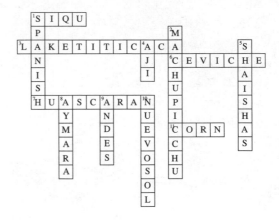

Page 40
1. b., 2. d., 3. c., 4. d., 5. b., 6. c., 7. b., 8. c.

Page 42
1. I, 2. E, 3. F, 4. H, 5. O, 6. B, 7. J, 8. G, 9. L,
10. N, 11. M, 12. K, 13. C, 14. A, 15. D.

Page 44
1. b., 2. c., 3. Alice Springs, 4. Melbourne,
5. Great Barrier Reef, 6. Perth, 7. Wyndham

Page 47
1. a., 2. b., 3. c., 4. a., 5. b., 6. a., 7. b., 8. b.

Answer Key

Page 48
1. K., 2. A., 3. N., 4. G., 5. D., 6. I., 7. L., 8. F.,
9. J., 10. B., 11. H., 12. C.

Page 50
1. d., 2. c., 3. a., 4. a., 5. b.

Page 51
Melanesia: New Guinea, Vanuatu, New Caledonia, Solomon Islands, Fiji
Micronesia: Guam, Caroline Islands, Mariana Islands, Gilbert Islands, Marshall Islands
Polynesia: Hawaiian Islands, Easter Islands Cook Islands, Midway Island, Marquesas Islands

Page 52

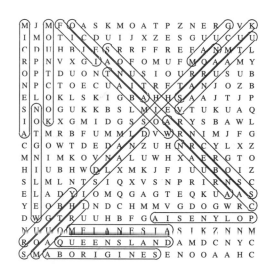

Page 54
1. N., 2. C., 3. F., 4. E., 5. M., 6. D., 7. B., 8. A.,
9. L., 10. J., 11. H., 12. I., 13. G., 14. K.

Page 56
1. d., 2. d., 3. c., 4. a., 5. b., 6. d., 7. d., 8. c.

Page 57
1. F, 2. T, 3. T, 4. F, 5. F, 6. T, 7. F, 8. F,
9. T, 10. F, 11. T, 12. F.

Page 59
1. b., 2. a., 3. c., 4. c., 5. a., 6. d.

Page 60

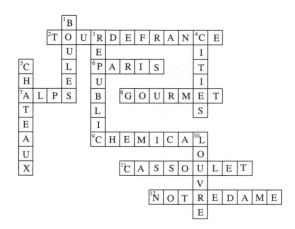

Page 62
1. d., 2. c., 3. b., 4. a., 5. d., 6. d.

Page 63

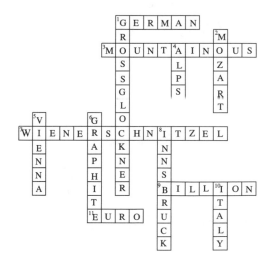

Answer Key

Page 65
1. c., 2. a., 3. b., 4. d., 5. a., 6. a.

Page 68
1. c., 2. c., 3. b., 4. a., 5. d.

Page 69

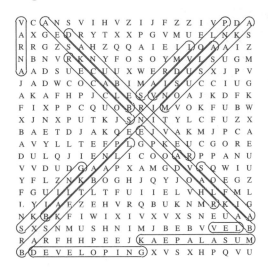

Page 71
1. c., 2. a., 3. d., 4. d., 5. c., 6. b.

Page 72
1. b., 2. c., 3. a., 4. c., 5. b.

Page 73
$100 = What is France's capital? What is Russia? What is Moscow? What is Austria? What is Sweden?
$200 = What is Italy? What is Sweden? What is Paris? What is Italy? What is Russia?
$300 = What is Sweden? What is France? What is Rome? What is France? What is Austria?
$400 = What is Russia's capital? What is Italy? What is Stockholm? What is Bulgaria? What is France?
$500 = What is Austria's capital? What is Bulgaria? What is Sofia? What is Sweden? What is Austria?

Page 73 (continued)
$600 = What is Bulgaria's capital? What is Austria? What is Russia? What is Italy?

Page 75
1. F., 2. O., 3. J., 4. L., 5. B., 6. G., 7. C., 8. K., 9. N,. 10. A., 11. I., 12. D., 13. E., 14. M., 15. H.

Page 77
1. c., 2. a., 3. a., 4. d., 5. c., 6. b.

Page 80
1. b., 2. c., 3. a., 4. d., 5. d., 6. c.

Page 81
1. c., 2. c., 3. c., 4. a., 5. c., 6. b.

Page 83
1. d., 2. d., 3. a., 4. b., 5. c., 6. d.

Page 84
NEW DELHI, BOMBAY, HIMALAYAS, THAR DESERT, DECCAN PLATEAU, GANGES, HINDUS, PULSES, CRICKET, FIELD HOCKEY, KITE FLYING, FILM INDUSTRY, SHAH JAHAN, TAJ MAHAL, DRAVIDIANS

LAND OF GREAT CONTRASTS AND VARIETY

Page 86
1. c., 2. a., 3. b., 4. d., 5. a.

Page 89
1. d., 2. b., 3. b., 4. c., 5. b., 6. d., 7. a.

Page 91
1. c., d.; 2. a., 3. a., c; 4. c.; 5. c.; 6. b.

Answer Key

Page 93
1. F., 2. H., 3. B., 4. A., 5. O., 6. D., 7. J., 8. K.,
9. I., 10. G., 11. N., 12. L., 13. M., 14. E., 15. C.

Page 95
1. b., 2. d., 3. b., 4. b., 5. b., 6. c.

Page 96
1. N., 2. A., 3. M., 4. B., 5. O., 6. C., 7. J., 8. G.,
9. K., 10. Q., 11. L., 12. P., 13. F., 14. D., 15. H.,
16. E., 17. I., 18. R.

Page 98
1. c., 2. d., 3. a., 4. b., 5. a.

Page 99

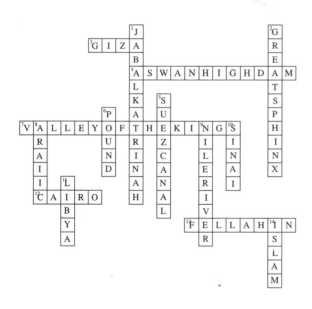

Page 101
1. c., 2. b., 3. d., 4. c., 5. b.

Page 104
1. c., 2. d., 3. d., 4. b., 5. a.

Page 105

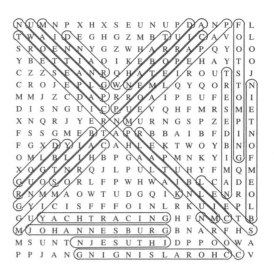

Page 107
1. d., 2. b., 3. d., 4. b., 5. d., 6. a.

Page 108
OMDURMAN, ARABIC, ISLAM,
LIBYAN DESERT, NUBIAN DESERT,
SUDD, BLUE NILE, KHARTOUM, FUL,
KISRA, GAMMONIA, MASCHI,
PORT SUDAN, MOUNT KINYETI

SUDAN IS THE LARGEST COUNTRY IN
SIZE IN AFRICA.

Page 110
1. c., 2. b., 3. c., 4. a., 5. d., 6. d.

Page 111
1. ELEPHANT, 2. GIRAFFE,
3. RHINOCEROS, 4. ZEBRA, 5. OSTRICH,
6. LION, 7. CHEETAH, 8. ANTELOPE,
9. LEOPARD, 10. BUFFALO,
11. HIPPOPOTAMUS, 12. EAGLE,
13. WARTHOG, 14. STORK

Answer Key

Page 114
1. b., 2. c., 3. a., 4. b., 5. c.

Page 115
1. b., 2. d., 3. d., 4. a., 5. c.

Page 116
1. ANTARCTIC CIRCLE
2. PLANKTON
3. SCIENTISTS
4. WILKES LAND
5. SOUTH POLE
6. VINSON MASSIF
7. GLACIERS
8. CONTINENTAL ICE SHEET
9. BLUE WHALE
10. ROSS SEA
11. PERMAFROST
12. WEDDELL SEA
13. ICE SHELF
14. ANTARCTIC PENINSULA

ANTARCTICA CONTAINS THE WORLD'S
LARGEST COLD DESERT

Pages 121–122
1. c., 2. b., 3. d., 4. c., 5. d., 6. a., 7. c., 8. a., d.;
9. c., 10. b., c., d.; 11. C., 12. N., 13. E., 14. B.,
15. O., 16. F., 17. I., 18. D., 19. A., 20. J., 21. H.,
22. K., 23. L., 24. G., 25. M., 26. H., 27. D.,
28. M., 29. J., 30. A., 31. O., 32. F., 33. B.,
34. K., 35. N., 36. E., 37. C., 38. L., 39. I., 40. G.,
41. F., 42. D., 43. J., 44. E., 45. C., 46. G., 47. A.,
48. H., 49. B., 50. I.